American Sweetheart

✪ *STILL* NOT MAKING THE TEAM ✪

By

CHIUFANG HWANG, M.D.

American Sweetheart: Still Not Making the Team Published November 2016

Editorial and proofreading services: Kathleen A. Tracy, Georgina Chong-you, Karen Grennan

Interior layout and cover design: Howard Johnson

Photo credits: All photographs are the sole owner of the author, Chiufang Hwang, M.D.

 SDP Publishing

Published by SDP Publishing, an imprint of SDP Publishing Solutions, LLC.

ISBN-13 (print): 978-0-9977224-5-1

ISBN-13 (ebook): 978-0-9977224-6-8

Library of Congress Control Number: 2016952474

Copyright 2016, Chiufang Hwang

Printed in the United States of America

Table of Contents

Introduction

On an early Saturday morning in April 1999, my alarm clock was set for 3:30 a.m. Before the first trill had fully sounded, I was instantly awake and out of bed. The moment I'd spent months training for was finally at hand. In just a few hours I'd literally be strutting my stuff at an audition for the Dallas Cowboys Cheerleaders—no matter that I'd never really even watched a football game on TV much less been to one. (The irony was not lost on me.)

Scurrying around my silent house like a bedazzled thief in the night, I put my hair in rollers, applied some makeup, grabbed my gym bag, and tiptoed out of the house into the crisp, North Central Plains night. My stealth wasn't only out of consideration for my sleeping family; my conservative husband had no idea his psychiatrist wife was trying out to be a cheerleader, and I preferred to keep it that way for the time being. You didn't need to be Freud to recognize that sometimes avoidance in a marriage can be a good thing.

The night was pitch black as I barreled down the Northwest Highway toward Texas Stadium in Irving. Fortunately, at that time West Dallas was teeming with sleazy strip clubs so when I got to that part of the highway I thought: *Perfect. At least I'm not alone.* Plus, the blinking lights made the road seem more festive than desolate.

As I passed by an assortment of fast food joints, I realized I was hungry. I had packed apples and other healthy snacks but that wasn't going to cut it. So I pulled into the Taco Cabana drive-thru and had to wait behind a line of cars. Who knew so many people were out getting food at that hour of the morning? Apparently watching strippers stimulates your appetite as well.

I finally got my tacos and was back on the highway. As I got closer to Texas Stadium, I had no idea what to expect once I got there. Two weeks earlier a local TV station, KDAF, had done a segment on me. This was back before reality TV made being unconventional a cottage industry, so a physician trying out to be a Dallas Cowboys Cheerleader was considered newsworthy. While I suspected they might want to do a follow-up story, I was not prepared for the media frenzy that surrounded the tryouts.

I pulled into the stadium at 5:30 a.m. thinking I'd be the first one there since the doors wouldn't open until nine o'clock. (Hey, you don't want an unexpected road closure or accident to ruin your pompom dreams.) Imagine my surprise to see the parking lot already full of cars. I remember thinking: *What is going on here?*

Through the DCC Looking Glass

My pre-dawn journey started with a letter from the DCC a few months earlier.

> *Dear Chiufang,*
> *Thank you for applying for the Dallas Cowboys Cheerleaders Auditions. Your completed application has been accepted and you are a Dallas Cowboys Cheerleaders Audition Candidate! Congratulations!*

The DCC staff was adamant I not be late and warned that I should expect to be there all day, dawn to dusk.

As if they could drag me out sooner. Clearly they didn't know who they were dealing with.

After parking I settled in, preparing to kill some time by eating. But in looking around I realized there were no bathroom facilities outside the stadium and the doors wouldn't open for several hours. So much for my taco ... or drinking water. I just stayed in my car and waited.

Around 6:30 a.m. the first few people started lining up. Since it was a first-come, first-served audition, I gathered my modest gym bag and got out to stand in line. In the five minutes it took me to get there, scores of other hopefuls had joined the queue. (I would officially be #94.) Standing in the cool morning as dawn broke, I checked out the women around me. They were all decked out in leotards and tights and had brought suitcases and wheelie bags filled with hair and makeup accessories. Many were accompanied by their mothers or friends. And most of them were gorgeous. It was like being at a beauty pageant. And I thought: *I am so out of place.* The fact I didn't really know how to dance was the least of it. *What am I doing standing in this line?*

But as the hours passed, the atmosphere became more vibrant, boredom morphing into nervous energy. Excitement was building and it was impossible not to get swept up by it. Then the media arrived and camera crews and print journalists started interviewing different women, asking where they were from. One was captain of a drill team from East Texas and another girl was a dance studio jazz instructor. Most of these girls were professional dancers. Many had driven in from out of state and were staying at the hotel across the street. The majority were also young. At thirty-four I was on the far end of the bell curve.

By the time they opened the doors, a line of six hundred women, plus their entourages, snaked around the stadium. As each participant entered, they matched you up with your application photo, then they took another photo of you and steered you to the Stadium Club. I'd never been in a VIP lounge before and I was definitely wowed and excited to get access to such a place. I thought it was very cool that you could see the field looking out the club's window.

The entire Stadium Club was filled with women preparing for

their moment. I just stood there absorbing the glitz, the activity, and the hum of anticipation—the room was practically vibrating. At the same time, I was getting more and more nervous as I watched the controlled chaos. Every electrical outlet was filled with plugs for hair dryers and curling irons. All around me were (super limber) girls practicing their routines, having their makeup expertly applied, or being combed, curled, teased, and tousled into big hair perfection.

I'm Taiwanese; big hair is not in our genes. There aren't enough curlers in the world.

I also worried I didn't have enough makeup on. But after a while those concerns became secondary to the thrill of being part of an event and the possibility of what could be. Even if only briefly, you belonged to a sorority very few people ever experience. While some of the girls clustered in cliques, I never felt there were any mean girls. Everyone was supportive of one another and friendly to me. I was on the floor stretching when one girl asked if I wanted a snack. I thought it was very cute.

Before the tryouts started they introduced the judges, a Texas entertainment industry hodge-podge that included one or two hairstylists, the director of the Cowboys' Cheerleaders, their choreographer, a couple of local news anchors, a dentist, a radio show host, and a DJ.

When it was show time, they sat you in rows and called you up in groups of five. Each group performed to different music and you didn't know what song you'd get for your two-minute audition. And even though they called it freestyle, it wasn't meant to be spontaneous. You're expected to have a choreographed routine that must include specific movements (kicks, splits, and other forms of joint torture) detailed on a spec sheet they had sent the applicants.

My number wasn't called until around noon. All morning I had kept practicing my routine to make it look like second nature, trying not to compare myself to the other girls who actually knew what they were doing. Then my group was up.

You're ushered in front of the judges, which was a bit nerve-wracking; there were bright lights on you so you can't really see the judges. And you knew that there were cameras everywhere recording you.

Someone said, "Introduce yourselves."

One girl was like, "I'm Susie Q, captain of the Apache Belles ..."

Another said, "I'm the head instructor of jazz at ..."

Then there was the one who had performed on Broadway.

(Sigh.)

When it was my turn I said my name, that I was a physician, and a mother of two sons. My palms were sweating so much I'm surprised I didn't leave a pool of water on the floor.

Then the music started. And I danced.

I wouldn't say I was self-conscious but I was very intimidated. And distracted. I couldn't help but look at the other girls who were kicking over their heads, whipping their heads in circles, twirling, and doing snake rolls. I became a bit of a spectator.

When the music stopped you were shooed off the stage, and the next group came on. It took all day, until almost six o'clock, to get through all the routines. I didn't mind. I was enthralled with the spectacle of it all. It was like being in Oz with a Texan twist. Two news reporters came up and interviewed me that day because I was definitely not your average applicant. I have to admit, I liked the attention I was getting and felt proud to represent women everywhere with a dream.

The atmosphere took a left turn when it was announced that the callbacks had been posted outside. Anxiety and a hint of desperation sucked the oxygen from the room. For many this was a make-it-or-break-it moment. Some of those girls had been dancing since they were three years old. They had been groomed for this. I had not, so my self-worth was not tied to the results.

The scene in front of the list was highly emotional. There were whoops and shrieks of joy and surprise mingled with the hysterical sobs from some who hadn't made it and infuriated stage mothers demanding to see the score sheets.

I did not make the cut, but I was not disappointed at all. I was inspired.

My immediate thought was: *I'm going to do this again next year. I'm going to train harder and get better and see what happens.* Besides it being a personal challenge, the camaraderie and shared sense of purpose I had experienced in those nine hours was an epiphany. I didn't miss having the friendship and camaraderie of teenage girlfriends in high school because I never knew what it was like to have it. But that day in Texas Stadium, I finally understood what I had missed out on in high school and college growing up as the eldest daughter of Taiwanese immigrants. I thought: *So this is what it's like.* I felt so special. I felt included. I felt more like a teenage girl than when I actually was one.

And I felt American. Because let's face it, there are few things more indigenously all-American than cheerleading.

Dallas Cowboys Cheerleading Audition Survival Kit

While not exactly embarking on the Appalachian Trail, the auditions are their own form of an endurance test. To make it through with spirits lifted, energy intact, and hair in place, you need to be prepared. My checklist includes:

★ A spare outfit or two. You don't want a wardrobe malfunction to ruin your big day, so bring more than one of everything, including shoes. Nothing says *I'm not ready for prime time—or the sideline* like a run in your hose while auditioning.

★ Water. Lots and lots of water. Everyone knows staying hydrated keeps the appearance of pesky wrinkles at bay.

★ Snacks. This could range from a mint for the size 2 crowd to trail mix, fruit, and protein bars. Save the cheeseburger for after your audition.

★ Rain gear. You don't want your 'do to get drenched in an unexpected downpour while waiting to enter the stadium.

★ Any and every beauty product item in your arsenal. Make up, curling iron, hair spray, styling mousse ... all to get that natural look.

★ Zen. Since there's no open bar to help quell your nerves, a calming state of mind helps you get past the surreal realization you are about to strut your stuff in front of six hundred professional dancers—and a television audience of millions.

★ Tissues. To hand to the emotional ladies who do, and don't, make the cut for the semi-finals.

★ Champagne split. To celebrate giving it your best.

Chapter 1

America's Sweethearts

Even though I grew up in America, I didn't have your typical American high school experience. No Texas *Friday Night Lights* experience for me. I might have been the only person in my school to graduate from high school without once ever attending a football game. Or basketball game. Or baseball game. To put it mildly, my mother kept me on a short cultural leash. More on that later.

While my first experience with trying out for the Dallas Cowboys cheerleaders—or DCC in the local lingo—didn't turn me into a football fan, it did make me fascinated with the whole cheerleading culture. Okay, maybe somewhat obsessed. It was like being admitted to a secret sorority I'd missed as a teenager, and I couldn't wait to experience it again. I also wanted to know more about the DCC in particular and cheerleading in general.

All those Friday nights spent studying at home might have made me a social outcast as a teen, but it also made me a world-class researcher. So when I'm interested in something I will research until I know everything about it. Cheerleading was no different. I find it ironic that an activity now so associated in the United States with females—whether in high school, college, or on the sideline at sports events—was actually an all-male pursuit back in the day. As in, back in the day before suffrage.

By the early 1900s, football was the most popular American college sport, and to cheer the players on, yell teams were formed. Mostly at Ivy League schools. I found a 1909 *New York Times* article that noted: "Strangers who see hatless and coatless youths making amazing gestures on the lawn in front of the big pavilion need not tremble for their safety. For the arm-waving, head-bobbing young men will be not maniacs, but cheerleaders."[1]

Seems like social controversy has always been a part of cheerleading. Two years later, Harvard's president, A. Lawrence Lowell, called cheerleading "the worst means of expressing emotion ever invented."[2]

The *Nation* magazine defended the activity as being right there alongside mom, apple pie, and Tom Brady. "The reputation of having been a valiant cheer-leader [sic] is one of the most valuable things a boy can take away from college. As a title to promotion in professional or public life, it ranks hardly second to that of being a quarterback."[3]

Not to be outdone by the East Coast elites, in 1924 Stanford introduced cheerleading to its curriculum. The *New York Times* reported: "There will be classes in bleacher psychology, correct use of the voice, and development of stage presence. Credit will be given to sophomores trying out for the position of yell-leader."[4]

By the end of the 1930s, more than 30,000 high schools and colleges had cheerleading squads. But World War II would bring widespread social changes. Not only did women fill manufacturing and other workplace jobs left vacant by men who enlisted or were drafted, they also started to take over cheerleading. After the war women were expected to go back to their *a-woman's-place-is-in-the-home* dynamic. But the cultural genie couldn't be put back in the bottle, and it could be argued that was when the seeds for the Women's Movement of the 1960s were planted. But there's little doubt the transition to female cheerleaders at colleges during the 1940s laid the foundation for women pursuing professional cheerleading.

In 1948 a former cheerleader named Lawrence Herkimer opened the first cheerleading camp; fifty-two girls and one boy attended that first year. The second year, 350 students participated. Six years later the Catholic Youth Organization held its first annual cheerleading competition for elementary, middle, and high school girls. In the early 1960s, 1,500 girls were competing. So by the time my family emigrated from Taiwan, cheerleading was part and parcel of many young girls' school experience—a rite of passage.

I suppose it was inevitable pro teams would see the value of having young women on the sidelines encouraging fans to root their team on. In 1970, eleven teams had cheerleading squads including the Atlanta Falcons' Falconettes, the Kansas City Chiefs' Chiefettes, and the Washington Redskins' Redskinettes. Clearly, coming up with catchy squad names wasn't a high priority.

While the Dallas Cowboys wasn't the first team to have cheerleaders, their squad would become by far the most famous. Mostly because Tex Schramm, general manager of the team, understood the value of entertainment. Put another way, he knew the public liked pretty girls.

Today, the young women who try out to be a DCC are athletes. Most have spent their lives studying dance or gymnastics. They are both strong and graceful. But back when Schramm wanted to reinvent his cheerleading squad, there was a bit of trial and error. At first he focused solely on appearance and hired professional models. It was not a pretty sight. After three hours jumping around in the Texas heat, the models straggled off the field looking more beat up than the players.

Next, he hired some local teenage dancers—they were still in high school—who were managed by a woman named Dee Brock. The new squad was named the CowBelles and Beaux. For more than a decade, the CowBelles cheered the Cowboys on, including their Super Bowl victory in 1971.

And no, I've never actually seen a Super Bowl either. Don't judge.

Anyway, before the start of the next season, Schramm had another idea and ran it past Dee. He wanted to take cheerleading Hollywood. Instead of high school kids, he wanted a squad of glamorous, accomplished dancers with choreographed routines that would be an attraction in their own right, beyond the game.

Dee hired dancer/teacher/choreographer Texie Waterman to set up auditions and put together a new squad. Depending on what article you read, the first audition attracted either sixty or one hundred hopefuls. To even get in the door you had to meet several requirements. Candidates had to be at least eighteen and either employed in a full-time job, enrolled as a full-time student, or a stay-at-home mom. Loafers need not apply.

The participants who passed that initial screening performed a two-minute routine in front of a panel of five judges, who then interviewed the ladies about football and the team. There were twenty finalists for the squad, all of whom fit the criteria: they could dance, had an all-American look, spoke well, and carried themselves with confidence.

Texie selected seven candidates, who spent the summer at a training camp. No more *Push 'em back, push 'em back, waaay back* with some enthusiastic jumping around. Texie's ladies learned routines filled with jetés, pirouettes, split jumps, and jazz hands.

The new faces of the Dallas Cowboys cheerleaders were Carrie O'Brien, Dixie Smith Luque, Anna Marie Carpenter Lee, Rosy Hall, Deanovoy Nichols, Dolores McAda, and Vonciel Baker, who had been the first black cheerleader at Texas Lutheran College.

An article I read in *Texas Monthly* quotes Carrie saying tryouts weren't as hard as she expected. "Most contestants wore white go-go boots and pranced around like Nancy Sinatra. I wore black boots and had a cap pistol that I pointed at the judges."[5]

Dallas introduced their new, improved squad at the start of the 1972 season. Gone were the CowBelles; in were the Dallas Cowboys ... Cheerleaders. Okay, still not the most creative name but I suppose it reflected a more professional approach. They were an immediate sensation. They performed choreographed routines in short shorts and tops that showed off their midriffs.

One prominent Cowboy was not at all pleased with the turn of events. Head coach Tom Landry did not want the cheerleaders on the sidelines. He did not consider them wholesome. I can't imagine the players' girlfriends and wives were overjoyed either. But the cheerleaders stayed, although Schramm made it clear these were professional performers and he expected them to act as such. The team implemented strict rules: no fraternizing with players or members of the Cowboys' staff, uniforms could only be worn at games or team-sponsored events, no smoking or drinking while in uniform, and squad members had to maintain their weight. As Schramm's secretary-turned-cheerleading director Suzanne Mitchell said in an interview I read: "We wanted everyone to look at them and say: *Now,* THEY *are ladies.*"[6]

Vonciel admitted the players didn't necessarily get the memo. "Before a game, one of the equipment boys knocked on our dressing room door and handed me a note. It was from a player we all know, but I'm not going to tell you who it was. It said: *Will you please meet me after the game? I'd like to take you to dinner.* I took the note and wrote on it: *Not in your lifetime!*"[7]

When Dee eventually left to get her graduate degree, Texie stepped in and became the Texas version of Mama Rose, raising her squad to even higher levels of creativity. Soon the DCC was becoming a burgeoning cottage industry. In addition to the hours spent rehearsing and in meetings, the DCC were sought after for personal appearances. Schramm asked Suzanne Mitchell to manage the squad in her spare time. It quickly became a full-time responsibility and in 1976 Mitchell became the first director of the Dallas Cowboys Cheerleaders.

If Texie was the chief creative officer behind the DCC, Suzanne was the CEO who developed the team into a worldwide brand. In Hollywood terms, their breakout moment came during the 1976 Super Bowl between Dallas and the Pittsburgh Steelers when they performed in front of three-quarters of a billion TV viewers around the world. The TV camera—or more accurately, the TV cameramen—couldn't get enough of them and were constantly showing close-ups of the squad between plays.

In 1977, *Esquire* featured the DCC on its cover with the tagline: *The Dallas Cowgirls (The Best Thing about the Dallas Cowboys)*. A year later, 475 hopefuls showed up to try out for the squad, which had grown to thirty-two members and four alternates. In 1979, more than one thousand women auditioned.

I can tell you from experience the amount of effort that goes into just auditioning. But those who make the squad train like professional athletes, which I guess they are. A 1978 *New York Times* article gave a glimpse into the life of a DCC team member.

"Stringent conditioning and diet control, rehearsals four or even five nights a week, five hours a night. Miss two rehearsals and you're off the squad forever. . . . Because of the strong Christian ethic that infuses the Cowboys program . . . the cheerleaders cannot appear where alcohol is served, cannot attend parties of any sort, cannot even wear jewelry with their brief costumes."[8]

The article also quoted some feminist groups who considered cheerleading demeaning, sexist, and exploitive. The *Times* writer noted, "With their short shorts, crop top, vest, and white boots, the Cowboy cheerleaders hardly resemble the spirited State U coeds of the past in long skirts and bobby socks."[9]

Some past DCC team members insinuated to the *Times* that as long as you had a D-cup, you were in. Suzanne took exception to that notion. "There is no emphasis on anything but sparkle," she stated.

"These girls are all different—even to their bodies. We're not looking for the same thing in every person."[10]

From what I've seen, I'd have to agree. I'd say it's dance ability first. If you don't have that, your bust size doesn't matter. And they want outgoing people who will engage fans. Everyone I've met at the auditions was either a student, working dancer or choreographer, or career woman. Nobody was being exploited. If anything, it's the opposite; most of the applicants I've met are looking to use the prestige of being a DCC to their advantage, either as a promotional opportunity or career stepping stone.

God knows it's not for the money. The 1977 article also reported that squad members earned fifteen dollars a game—$14.72 after taxes—and weren't paid for practice. Well, not much has changed on that front. Today's squad members make fifty dollars a game—they probably spend that much in hair spray—and they still don't get paid for the hours spent rehearsing.

And it's also not about making a career of being a DCC. The average life span of a Cowboys cheerleader is only two to three years. All that hard work for a brief moment in the sideline sun. The high attrition rate is directly related to the schedule, which includes nightly rehearsals from 7:00 to 10:30 p.m. Some call it demanding; I would say grueling because most of the ladies on the team are either in college or have full-time jobs during the day so they can, you know, afford to buy food and not have to live in their car. The time commitment not only takes a physical toll on the team members but impacts their personal and family lives as well.

Obviously, it's the side benefits that make being a DCC so sought after: prestige, modeling opportunities, personal appearances, and now TV exposure in the reality cable show *Dallas Cowboys Cheerleaders: Making the Team.* Many former cheerleaders go on to open their own dance studios using the DCC credential to attract business, especially young girls who dream of being on the sidelines one day wearing the blue and white.

One of the more successful former DCC is an actress named Sarah Shahi (*The L Word, Person of Interest, Drew*), who grew up in Texas. "Everyone knew I wanted to be an actress, so they said: *Why don't you try out for the Cowboys Cheerleaders?* Back in 1995 they were on *Saturday Night Live* so I figured that could be my way in; I tried out just to get on *SNL*."[11]

While making the squad didn't get her to New York, it was her ticket to California after a chance meeting with director Robert Altman, who was shooting scenes for one of his films at the cheerleader rehearsal facilities. "He took me under his wing," Shahi says. "One day he asked me what I wanted to do, and I said: *I want to be an actress.* He said: *Then you should move to LA. I think you have what it takes.* And that's what I did."[12]

Dallas won the Super Bowl again in 1978. In the NFL's highlight film of the Cowboys' championship season, the narrator referred to them as *America's team.* The term stuck. And soon the DCC were known as America's sweethearts. Considering that I lived in Texas and never heard of them as a teenager shows you just how isolated I was from American pop culture because a casual search online shows that they were everywhere in the late 1970s. That '77-'78 squad appeared on NBC's *Rock-n-Roll Sports Classic* and an Osmond Brothers special on ABC. They appeared in a shampoo commercial and kicked off the '78 season hosting their own one-hour special (*The 36 Most Beautiful Girls in Texas*) before the first Monday Night Football game of the season. They also appeared in a two-hour made for TV movie (*The Dallas Cowboys Cheerleaders*) starring Jane Seymour that aired in January 1979, followed by a sequel a year later.

Texie retired in 1983 and Suzanne quickly hired Shannon Baker Werthmann. A former DCC team member, Shannon was Texie's protégé and had been working as her assistant. She stayed for ten years. During that time the DCC began their collaboration with the USO to perform for American military troops stationed overseas.

By the time I started trying out, the current team of Kelli McGonagill Finglass and Judy Trammell were in charge, carrying the torch lit by Suzanne and Texie. Both ladies have risen through the high-kicking ranks of the DCC.

Judy was a Cowboys cheerleader from 1980–84, followed by six years as the squad's assistant choreographer. She's been the head choreographer since 1991.

Kelli was on the squad for five years (1984–89) and has the distinction of being the only cheerleader in DCC history to be invited back (by Suzanne Mitchell) for her fifth season without having to go through the customary audition process. After hanging up her pom-poms, Kelli then spent a year in the Cowboys' sales and promotions department and another year as the squad's assistant director before taking over. She is regularly described as a combination of mediator, consultant, administrator, and disciplinarian.

Apparently, it's not just Texas you don't mess with.

From the moment I entered the facility for the audition, it was clear Finglass and Trammell ran a tight ship. And I appreciate that. I get being disciplined. Without it, you wouldn't accomplish much. But even though the auditions are organized and participants are expected to act professionally, it's not like boot camp. It's also fun with a lot of camaraderie and a sense you're a part of something special that few get to experience. That effort to put your best foot forward and give it all you've got is addictive.

You can tell that in Kelli's mind the Dallas Cowboys Cheerleaders are more than just performers. They are everywoman. To that end she says what they look for in their hopefuls is a cross section of American women. They are looking for savvy role models who bring the entire package: community involvement, poise, attractiveness, confidence, and of course talent. Kelli views the opportunity to be a Dallas Cowboys Cheerleader as a gift that is meant to be shared with both the community and fans. So cheering on the sideline is only part of the responsibility. Each lady needs to be relatable to everyone, from young children to seniors, and they have to represent the Cowboy organization, the players, and the city in what Finglass calls a first-class manner.

"The organization affords them an opportunity to broaden their own lives and enrich the lives of others as they travel throughout the United States and around the world. They are given a perspective on life that they may not have considered before. And that might lead them to reassess what's truly important ... and to share that with others."[13]

One former DCC credits her time on the team with giving her confidence and a positive attitude she parlayed into a successful post-cheerleader professional and personal life. "Regardless of what the football players and other people in the organization do or don't do, the squad still abides by its strict guidelines, and I'm so proud of that. There was a little criticism in the beginning, but I think that was because the organization was misunderstood. They might have pioneered NFL cheerleading, but the legacy is much more."[14]

Speaking of legacy, those original seven squad members are still considered icons within the Cowboys organization. They were the pioneers that ushered in the modern DCC. Every so often a magazine will seek them out to see what they're up to. Most went on to successful careers.

Carrie O'Brien played on the US women's soccer team for five years then became a regional sales representative for Dale Tiffany lamps in Dallas.

Anna Marie Carpenter Lee was dean of women at Tyler Junior College and director of the Apache Belles.

Rosy Hall, sister of model Jerry Hall who was married to Mick Jagger, moved to London to be near her sister and established herself as a fashion designer.

Dixie Luque proved to be a natural-born salesperson for a residential building company.

Vonciel Baker took to the skies as a flight attendant. "I went from cheerleading for the Cowboys to cheerleading for Southwest."

Deanovoy Nichols landed in customer service for a telecom.

In 2001, they had a reunion in the pages of *Texas Monthly*. A few still worked out religiously to keep their DCC figures. Dixie said she regularly lifted weights, took Jazzercise and aerobics classes, drank her eight glasses of water, and favored fish and vegetables.

Did I mention that immediately following my tryout routine I went in desperate search of a cheeseburger? But I digress.

Anna Marie reported she ran two miles four times a week, did fifteen minutes on a stair climber, and lifted weights for half an hour. "I love to eat," she explained. "My husband and I belong to a gourmet club. Exercise balances that out." Vonciel had done her time at the gym. "Listen, after dancing that long in that heat in Texas Stadium, there's no way I'm going to work out or diet again. I eat what I want. And I know how to make a mean margarita."[15]

Reading about the history of the Dallas Cowboys Cheerleaders gave me an even greater appreciation for the organization. And a clearer understanding of why I'm so drawn to the extravaganza—the show—that is DCC tryouts. I'm an immigrant and I'm an American. I grew up feeling stuck in one culture while longing to be part of the other. Don't get me wrong; I love my Taiwanese culture. But I also love the opportunity to push the envelope just for the hell of it. To put in months of work for the sheer thrill of making it through a two-minute dance routine without falling or giving myself whiplash. It is exhilarating. The women who try out for the DCC prove that you can be both professional and flashy. You can be a responsible wife and mother while allowing yourself the freedom for improbable pursuits. It's not either/or.

It wasn't until that first tryout that I realized the importance of having a guilty pleasure. I truly have no expectation of making the team; for me it's about the journey of getting there every year, the months of challenging myself to get stronger, learning to be a better dancer, and knowing that I've improved with each audition. It's a unique sense of accomplishment.

I won't lie; I also love the attention of the judges, the other participants, and the media. As I said before, it has given me a sense of belonging in my adopted culture that I was so isolated from as a kid. Exactly why I grew up always feeling I was on the outside looking in was a perfect storm of family circumstances, innate shyness, and an Asian culture that placed academic achievement above all other pursuits.

Q & A with Kelli Finglass [16, 17, 18]

What's the biggest stereotype about the cheerleaders?

I think a lot of times the people don't realize that the cheerleaders have careers and have impressive educations. All of our cheerleaders have their bachelor's degrees and ten have their master's degree, while some are still enrolled at various universities. Last year we had a cheerleader with her doctorate. So the old stereotype is that cheerleaders aren't as educated, but that really couldn't be anywhere further from the truth. From doctors and lawyers to sales personnel and school teachers, our cheerleaders have some very impressive careers.

What's it like being a cheerleader?

Well, it's a whirlwind. It's a very busy lifestyle; a fabulous collection of friends and dancers and athletes. For performers it's really a dream come true to be able to perform and dance, and then you mix that with the NFL and it's an amazing experience. The best part is probably the close friendships that develop through the camaraderie of the travels and the locker room.

The experiences that they have together, for example, through trips like this to the Riviera Maya; imagine going to an area like this for eight days with twenty-one of your best friends. It's just an incredible, fun, exciting, glamorous, and exotic adventure.

You've called the tryouts and uniform sacred. Do you really see it that way?

For those of us that are in marketing and branding and the

business side of it, this uniform is recognized worldwide. It was a very strong brand with great qualities to it. And so for that reason, sacred to some might seem dramatic. But for fans that come to the Dallas Cowboys' games and have seen just the star on the Cowboys helmet, to be inside the stadium, to see a football player for the first time in person, to see a cheerleader in person ... because it's so well-recognized, because it's a symbol of excellence, it's special. It's magical. It is a part of the excitement of the National Football League, and for the people that have worn it, yes, we would say it's sacred.

What would be the number one thing you would like people to know about the DCC?

Probably how impressive the girls are as individuals and collectively as a group, how close they really are. Sometimes people think that a group of women might not get along well, and that's the furthest thing from the truth. They are very close friends and become almost like family. They have impressive educations, impressive careers. And after they're cheerleaders they not only go on to have families and have wonderful careers, but they have been and will always be ambassadors for the Dallas Cowboys.

Chapter 2

Definitely Not the Typical Girl Next Door

My parents emigrated from Taiwan in 1968 when I was two years old so my father could earn his PhD, a pursuit that would consume his time, attention, and money for the next two decades. The first place we lived was the small town of Hempstead, Texas, near Prairie View A&M University, where my father had been hired to teach math. We rented one of several cottages on a farm located right off the highway and shared the property with farm hands, ranch employees, and snakes that flourished in the wildly overgrown grass. A few months later we jumped on the highway in my father's decrepit, blue Plymouth to Prairie View and settled into a boxy fourplex sandwiched between a Greyhound depot and a gas station.

Our next stop in 1969 was Rock Hill, South Carolina, where my father was a teacher at Friendship College. My mother worked a few hours a day without pay at the college in exchange for free board in a trailer parked on campus between the women's dorm and the office of the math department dean.

We didn't go out much except to the student rec room or the dining hall. At night my mother and I worked on jigsaw puzzles of American landscapes like Yosemite, the Grand Canyon, and the giant sequoias. And I had math workbooks to keep me busy. Part of my parents' way of showing love was to groom me to be a good student. My mother would make ten copies of each workbook and have me work on them one after another over the course of a month until I got a perfect score. She also drilled me on multiplication tables, which put me way ahead in math.

We lived in that trailer until it went up in flames after its propane tank caught fire. I remember watching it burn and being afraid because we had no place to go.

Needless to say, my earliest memories of the United States weren't exactly the stuff of dreams.

In 1970 my father was accepted into the mathematics PhD program at the University of South Carolina, so we moved—again—to Columbia, an hour south of Rock Hill. Our new home was in a low-income housing project that looked like an Army barracks. That is where I would spend my formative years.

Our neighbors were either white or African-American. No Hispanics. At that time in the towns where we lived, Asians were rare and considered somewhat exotic. In second grade I made the front page of the *Columbia Record* just because I was one of only two Asians who had started school that year. (Our fathers were both graduate students.) I have to admit, I loved seeing myself in the newspaper and in a strange way, it made me feel validated. I was someone worth paying attention to.

My parents enrolled me in first grade when I was five. Everybody else was already reading fluently while I could barely manage Dick, Spot, and Jane. We spoke only Taiwanese at home so I was way behind. I was also often left behind. The school wasn't walking distance and didn't have buses, and my father wasn't exactly what you'd call prompt.

On one of my first grade report cards the teacher wrote: "Chiufang cries every afternoon. Perhaps some reassurance that you will pick her up will help out."

When I wasn't in school, my father used the library for childcare. He'd drop me off around 7:45 in the morning at a math and engineering library in the building where the computer science and engineering departments were located. He instructed me to stay put then rushed off to his 8:00 a.m. class.

By the time he picked me up at noon, I was starving. My father would take me to a diner on campus and buy himself a burger and fries and a kid's meal for me. Compared to my mother's home cooking, my little burger was heaven.

He'd drop me back at the library by 12:45, and I'd be there until he came back between 5:00 and 6:00 p.m. My father never asked me what I did all day. No one else asked me what I was doing there, although people sometimes stared at this tiny girl, not even four feet tall, alone all day in a library with adults.

My first week there I prowled around looking for something to do. I discovered the *Encyclopedia Britannica*, which was my best friend throughout those long summer vacations from school.

Eventually my parents realized they needed more formal childcare. I needed somewhere to stay both before and after school, but in 1972 where we lived, there were no after-school programs, no child-care centers. My mother had to leave home at 6:30 a.m. to catch the bus to her minimum wage factory job and wouldn't get home until six o'clock that night. My father went to school for his PhD during the day and worked the graveyard shift at a convenience store. Since my mother didn't speak English, I had to go around to the neighbors and find someone who would watch me. My first babysitters were Mr. and Mrs. Chavis. I negotiated a rate of a dollar a day. They had three children, and I grew to love their family. The atmosphere was lively with activity and conversation. I soaked it up. The coolest thing at the Chavises' house was watching TV, which my family did not have.

I ate dinner with them every evening, and that's where I became acquainted with collard greens, black-eyed peas, hominy grits, biscuits, okra, fried chicken, and cornbread. Southern food became my immediate favorite. As I mentioned, my mother's cooking was, let's say ... *challenged.* Our typical meal was white rice with beef chunks, green beans, and greasy gravy. Sometimes we had cabbage. This was not Taiwanese food or any country's recognizable cuisine. This is why when home I feasted on Cap'n Crunch cereal whenever possible.

The Chavises might not have been educated or sophisticated, but for the year and a half I spent with them, they were the best family I ever had.

☆☆☆

My brother Chi-Cheng was born when I was in first grade, nearly six years old, and I was so excited that now I had this real, live, little baby doll to play with. I'd been the only child for so long, and I was overjoyed from the first moment I saw him. In the Chinese tradition, I called him *little brother* instead of his given name, and when he learned to talk, he called me older sister.

Even as a six-year-old second grader I realized it was my job to care for my parents as far as daily life. I acted as intermediary with neighbors, babysitters, and landlords; translated; wrote school letters and filled out forms; hired babysitters; and after my brother—and later, my sister—was born, became a surrogate parent. I was tightly scheduled and at my parents' beck and call, never free to come and go. It was stressful. Plus, my parents' work took priority over anything I wanted to do. They never saw that as interfering with my life, but it did.

I knew I was indispensable but rarely felt appreciated. In a Chinese family, whether in the US or back home in Taiwan, you don't *say* you love somebody, you *show* it, but never conspicuously. The principle is that you don't need to tell a person something that's obvious. But sometimes we desperately need to hear those obvious things. It's good for the soul.

At the time I wasn't really cognizant of juggling cultures. It was just the way things were. I had no choice but to accept the responsibility given me.

Since I didn't get out much, I was on the frail side as a little girl. I'd often get dizzy. I was not very nimble or flexible. So it's not too surprising that I wasn't very good at sports or outdoor children's games. It was kind of a chicken or the egg scenario. Maybe I wasn't athletic—or even coordinated—because my parents stressed academics and very much discouraged sports or outdoor activities. Plus, they wanted me to be feminine and skinned knees were way too tomboyish for their sensibilities. So while other kids played outside, I was at the kitchen table writing out checks to pay our bills.

☆☆☆

My father's efforts to earn his PhD in Columbia didn't pan out after he failed the verbal defense of his dissertation and was dropped from the program. He sent out countless letters to various universities looking for employment and to secure a new doctorate program. I was nine years old and in the middle of fifth grade when I found out we were moving to Birmingham, where my father had been accepted into the University of Alabama's computer science PhD program. In his mind, this was going to be our final move.

We were leaving between Christmas and New Year, so that December I said my goodbyes to teachers, babysitters, and those I called friends. In reality, I never really had any true friends, but in my mind I always considered any person I spent time with—even a short time—my friend. I felt very connected to individuals in my environment.

We loaded everything into a Ryder truck, which one of my father's students agreed to drive for us, while my four-year-old brother, my nine-month-old sister, my parents, and me were in our car. I remember wishing we didn't have to go.

It was snowing when we arrived in Birmingham. As in, near white-out conditions snowing. And it turned out we had no place to go. My parents had not seen the value of renting an apartment in advance. They decided we'd just drive around near the university and find an apartment once we got there.

You really can't make this stuff up.

Suffice it to say, braving snowdrifts taller than me, I made sure my parents took the first apartment we found, which was actually quite nice compared to our last place. We unpacked and settled in.

I was still homesick when I started my new school. Being the new girl in class was hard for a shy kid like me, especially being the smallest, the youngest, and the only Asian. As if I didn't feel out of place enough as it was, my Birmingham classmates were miles ahead of me in reading. Turned out public schools in Alabama were much more advanced than those in South Carolina. Fortunately, I was still ahead in math. My father made sure of that.

He really was an excellent math teacher. Even though he struggled in his own academic pursuits, he made sure I and my siblings would shine in *his* subject. During every school break he gave us assignments. And I mean every break: Christmas vacation, spring recess, national holidays, and our entire summer vacation. I finished a math textbook that was far above my grade level within six weeks. I thought: *This is great! I get July and August off.*

I thought wrong.

My father had other plans; he just gave me a second textbook. "You'll learn it better this way," he said happily, "because you'll get a different perspective on the subject from another publisher."

After just a few weeks at my new school, I was excelling in social studies as well, and had memorized all the state capitals. I also became the teacher's pet, and the attention made me feel validated and good about myself. (Clearly, I haven't changed much in that regard.)

Things were looking up for me in Birmingham. But just as I was starting to feel at home in our new city, we abruptly had to leave. For whatever reason, my father was dropped from the graduate program. Either he was booted out, or he decided that the program wasn't right for him. He never said. So we packed back up and returned to South Carolina. We'd been gone just eight weeks.

During sixth-grade, I started riding city buses all over using my student pass and would spend every weekday afternoon from 3:30 to 6:30 wandering the streets of Columbia. My parents had no idea where I was after school and never asked. I kept my new-found independence under the radar (a skill I would hone over my lifetime that would serve me well thirty years later when I started auditioning to be a Dallas Cowboys cheerleader).

By that time we had a TV, and while watching shows was fun sometimes, exploring my world was fun all the time—even though not every part of Columbia was kid friendly. Or people friendly. At some of the bus stops, I was the only passenger who got off. The bus drivers started recognizing me and seemed to be keeping an eye on me. I'm sure they thought I was either a homeless orphan or a midget drug mule because I did not remotely look my age. As a ten-and-a-half-year-old sixth grader, I was a tick over four feet tall and very slender. I'm sure I could have passed for a six-year-old.

But my diminutive size led to one of my closest childhood friendships. Janine Hutchinson was a heavyset, black girl in my science class who also rode the city bus. The first time she saw me on the bus, she came over and plopped down next to me. I liked her; she was friendly and funny.

From that day on, Janine always wanted to ride with me. She was afraid I would get kidnapped and was protective of me. So she became my personal body guard.

Janine promised, "Anybody want to mess with you, they gotta

mess with me first. I'm gonna stick with you on this bus." She couldn't always ride with me, but she tried to follow wherever I went.

In some ways, Janine reminded me of Lisha Tucker, another self-appointed bodyguard who had looked out for me in elementary school. Those friends were typical of my survival instinct. I didn't pick regular friends.

Janine and I were an odd pair; she was nearly a foot taller and eighty pounds heavier but we adored each other. With Janine by my side, downtown Columbia—and its colorful, bath-challenged denizens—seemed less threatening. On the bus, Janine kept up a running, irreverent commentary about the other passengers, making me laugh uncontrollably.

Janine was determined to teach me how to dance like a black person. "White people can't move!" she declared, then showed me how it was done. "This way ... swing your ass, girl."

I couldn't do it very well, but I tried. And yes, more than once I've thought of Janine as I stood in front of the DCC judges, thinking what a kick she'd get out of me showing my moves.

My parents knew nothing about my best friend, and she never came over to visit. But one day Janine brought me to her grandfather's house. He had a gigantic collection of Motown records and wanted to give me an armful, but I took only one album.

Riding with Janine was the best part of any day.

My sister Mingfang was born in April, 1975, when I was in fourth grade. Once while we were visiting family friends, she was playing quietly by herself on the floor when she fainted. It took many minutes for my parents to wake her up. As a toddler we noticed she bruised very frequently, then around the time we returned to Columbia she became lethargic, as if chronically tired. But my parents never considered these strange symptoms worrisome enough to have her checked out.

Then one night she started convulsing while we were having dinner. We rushed her to the emergency room. It was an unbearably frantic, terrifying drive way across town. She was so listless I thought she was dead. The hospital admitted her immediately. My parents followed as they took her in. My brother and I were left behind and waited. We eventually fell asleep in a chair. My father came out at midnight to take us home. My mother stayed.

The next day my father told me Mingfang had suffered a simple febrile seizure brought on by leukemia. Acute lymphocytic leukemia to be exact. They couldn't cure her, but they could treat her disease and prolong her life. There was no way we could afford treatment; we had no insurance. Fortunately, my sister's care would be covered under Medicaid.

My sister has cancer.

I dwelled on that new reality. It brought home, in a very personal way, that life can be short and nothing is guaranteed. There may not be a tomorrow, so if you want something don't put it off. Attack life with all the purpose you can muster. We can't let others' opinions or negativity stop us from striving for goals big and small. Yes, be responsible, but don't be afraid to go after a dream, however improbable or whimsical it may be. Don't let shyness or worry about failing get in the way of trying new experiences. I didn't know it then at eleven, but looking back now I can see what a profound impact my sister's diagnosis had on my developing view of life and my place in it.

My sister remained in the hospital for a week and a half. After she was stabilized, they transferred her to the Medical University of South Carolina in Charleston, where she received radiation treatment as an inpatient. We didn't see her or my mother until three months later at Christmas.

You might wonder how my mother managed to communicate with hospital staff. She didn't. She simply let the hospital staff do what they needed to do to save her child. No interpretation was needed.

☆☆☆

Not long after bringing my sister and mother back home from Charleston, my father announced we were moving again. This time to College Station, Texas, in pursuit of his latest goal. Texas A&M's College of Engineering had accepted him into its computer science PhD program. So once again around Christmas we were packing up our lives and saying goodbyes.

Not only was I leaving school in the middle of seventh grade, the move meant my bus-riding adventures were suddenly over. As was my time with Janine, my protector. I waited until we were sitting together on the bus on my last day before telling her. We both cried and cried. We had never lived anywhere long enough for me to form close friendships, except for Janine. So leaving was hard on me. But it's always harder on the one left behind. She wailed, heartbroken and worried about who was going to protect me. We corresponded for months after I moved. In her long, long, handwritten letters, she told me how much she missed me. I dearly loved my friend Janine.

We never saw each other again.

☆☆☆

On moving day, we loaded everything into a U-Haul by ourselves, hitched it to the back of our old car, and spent three long days driving to Texas. I had expected warm weather but we saw plenty of ice and snow. We arrived in College Station on New Year's Day and spent the first night in a Motel 6.

Mercifully, I didn't have to negotiate a new apartment lease for my family. The university provided us low-rent, married-student housing—a furnished, five hundred square foot, one-bedroom apartment. It was ... cozy. Good thing I didn't take up much room. Eventually, they moved us to a two-bedroom.

As soon as we arrived in College Station, my mother started taking Mingfang to Texas Children's Hospital in Houston, where doctors would draw blood and administer whatever treatments or follow-up procedures they felt were needed. The monthly trips continued for almost two years, then went down to once each quarter, then finally twice a year for the rest of her life. Adding stress to the situation was my parents' insistence that my sister's illness remain a secret, so I was forbidden to talk about it. They worried that if other Asian families found out, nobody would want to marry me because I might have bad genes.

My genes were just fine; my parents should have been much more worried about my fitness. I enrolled in A&M Consolidated Middle School to finish out seventh grade. Not long after I arrived, we had to participate in a state fitness test. To pass you needed to run a mile in twenty minutes. I couldn't. Do a certain number of sit-ups in one minute. I could barely do two. Do a chin hold for sixty seconds. I couldn't even hold my body weight. Obviously, I didn't pass and that was more than a little humiliating.

In school and around the student housing complex, I had plenty of opportunities to see other families and now that I was older I began to notice the differences between their family and mine. For one, American parents openly showed their children lots of affection. Even more obvious to me was that their children were children. They seemed ... freer.

I felt my purpose was to take care of both parents, especially my mother. Not just paperwork and translating; by 4:00 p.m. every day, I took over all childcare duties for the next three hours. I made sure they ate, supervised their homework, and got them to bed. Only then, during the school year, would I be able to study and do homework. I was twelve; my brother, six; my sister, three.

Doing this every day drove me nuts. It made me want to run away, and so I did. Literally. The minute my father came home, I was out the door. At first, I would just walk around the Texas A&M campus to clear my head and relieve the tension. After a while I started jogging, and gradually started running—all in my cheap tennis shoes. Besides being an emotional outlet, running made me stronger.

In eighth grade I passed the fitness test. My sense of accomplishment was like the best runners' high ever.

The school year went by fast and soon everyone was anticipating the year-end dance. It wasn't a couples' event; it was basically a class celebration. Planning for the event started back in September, and as the school year wound down, giant banners promoting the dance papered the school halls. The school was abuzz and everyone was going.

Except me. Earlier that fall, I'd told my mother about the festivities being planned for spring, explaining, "It's not just a party. It is the culmination of middle school and eighth grade and it symbolizes a milestone. We're all going on to the next stage, high school. This is important for everybody in school."

My mother forbid it. There was nothing I could do to change her mind. She never gave me a reason why she would keep a kid from participating in their once-in-a-lifetime celebration, especially since there was not going to be a formal graduation. Once again I felt like a complete outsider as everyone was eagerly anticipating the dance.

One day a girl on the Banner Committee asked me to help out, since I'd taken art classes and had won several awards at juried art shows for watercolor and landscape. I was so flattered that she would ask me but had to decline because I couldn't attend.

My mother took away my party. The night of the dance I cried. Home alone.

☆☆☆

Like other teenagers in the university community, I entered A&M Consolidated High School. Life was stable, for now. I studied, took care of my parents and siblings, and ran. At the end of my freshman year, I participated in Field Day at school, still in my old tennies, and competed in the 880—a half-mile race, two laps around the track.

Having no knowledge of proper running strategy, I blasted off as fast as I could, all the while hearing people call out, "Chiufang, pace yourself! You're starting too fast!"

But I ignored them and continued my loops around the track. When I crossed the finish line I was astonished to see I'd left all the other kids behind. That first-place win was an unbelievable thrill and also got the attention of the cross-country coach, who asked me to join the school's team. That honor made me so very happy; I, of course, accepted. Since practice started in seventh period it didn't involve me asking my mother for permission. I didn't have to ask her to drive me anywhere and because it was during school hours in the afternoon, it took place before the time she mandated I be at home to watch my brother and sister.

I had developed painful shin splints from running in bad shoes. Luckily for me, shoe vendors frequently gave pairs of shoes to track coaches so that runners could try them out so I switched to real running shoes with cushioned padding and strong arch supports. Running became my primary social outlet.

I was not allowed to attend the Sadie Hawkins dances, homecoming, any sporting events, or even movies. *Close Encounters, Star Wars,* and *Carrie* came and went as I missed out on the culture of my youth. Everyone was imitating characters from those films, but all the references were lost on me.

I was nowhere near as image-conscious as most high-school girls because I couldn't be. I was not allowed to wear makeup or spend any money on nice clothes. I didn't grow much, so in high school I still wore clothes from my sixth-grade days in Columbia. My "wardrobe" never really wore out.

For so long growing up I was only given one path to follow by my parents: academics and medical school. My mother made sure that I was studying all the time. The social aspect of high school wasn't part of my accepted culture—unless it was academic, like the science or math club. But I got a taste of it with cross-country because I got to be around girls my own age. We had fun but we also seriously trained. We had to run like five miles a day and we had to hit certain numbers. I loved how regimented the program was. And you can eat anything you want and not worry about gaining weight. A total win-win.

But my high school running career was cut short. My father was sure he would finally get his doctorate and was applying for jobs. Midwestern State University in Wichita Falls, Texas, offered him a position for the following academic year, with the contract renewal contingent on securing his PhD. The plan was that he would teach in Wichita Falls and come back to College Station once a month to meet with his advisor and complete his dissertation.

So we moved three hundred miles north to Wichita Falls and I started over again. I was very lonely at my new high school in the beginning. Arriving as a junior was just about the worst time to start. All the other kids had formed bonds with each other over the years. Most of my classmates were middle-class white kids, children of Midwestern faculty members and military kids from nearby Sheppard Air Force Base. I'd never been in a school where so many kids paid full price for lunch.

And academically they were accustomed to a much brisker pace of learning than I was accustomed to. Even in math class, where I'd really stood out at A&M Consolidated, I was just average because they had been in advanced classes.

The science curriculum was all new to me, too. In biology, I knew nothing about nomenclature, while my classmates could recite the genus and species of each plant, insect, and animal we were studying. Although I devoted extensive time to catching up and memorizing, I barely made a B on my first report card.

Worst of all was English class, which focused on writing. I plugged away diligently but my writing skills were undeveloped so I only earned a C for my efforts. At least before I could always hold onto my academic achievements when I felt left out. But during the year I spent in Wichita, I didn't even have that solace as I sat on the figurative sidelines while my classmates were enjoying football games, pep rallies, and the fall dance.

That spring, the nice boy who sat in front of me in math class asked me to prom. There were no romantic overtures; it was just to have a fun night. Of course my mother said no and at that point I would never challenge her.

Despite my lack of extra-curricular participation, I had begun to enjoy S.H. Rider High School. I was able to take Drivers' Ed, which was mandatory, and it offered a better all-around education. I had also made some friends. So imagine my angst when my father failed to get his PhD and Midwestern did not renew his teaching contract.

We were going back to College Station. I was especially disappointed because I liked Midwestern State University, its library, and its compact campus. My mother had already decided that I'd be going to Midwestern, but now that was impossible because I was required to live at home during my college years.

When I announced that I was moving away, the kids in my science class arranged a big surprise for me. They had all signed a yearbook—bought by a boy named Brady—and the teacher presented it to me in front of the class. I was so shocked and touched. I never really knew my benefactor. He sat about three rows away from me in class. I struggled to hold back tears.

I returned to A&M Consolidated High School for my senior year but after a year away, things had changed. My former pals were no longer friends, and in the cafeteria I sat with ninth-graders. I didn't try out for the cross-country team again. It was really time consuming, and my grades had dropped a little bit when I was on the team because by the time you got home you were so tired you didn't have as much energy to study in what time you did have.

I graduated from high school at seventeen. It wasn't a particularly momentous occasion. There was no celebration. No wild cheering from my family when I walked across the stage to receive my diploma. No graduation parties shared with friends. It was like I had grown up in an alternate universe, able to see another way of living but unable to truly experience it. Except vicariously. And it left a bit of a void in me and a yearning.

What the Dallas Cowboys cheerleading tryout experience gives me is an entrée into the inner lives of these other ladies who grew up so differently from me. For those few hours, I get to see, breathe, and feel what it's like to be these other people in a way. And I get something positive out of that.

But I would have never been able to immerse myself in my DCC pursuit, or have the freedom to be myself, if I hadn't managed to cut the dependency cord with my mother. And there was only one sure way to do that.

Everything You Need to Know about the Dallas Cowboys Cheerleader Auditions.

★ Don't expect to get rich and retire. While being a DCC is in reality a full-time job because of the rehearsal requirements, it pays like a high school part-time job at a fast-food joint. Plus, most of those trying out—and on the squad for that matter—have either full-time jobs or are college students.

★ Being a DCC is not just for all the single ladies. There have been quite a few moms over the years.

★ Unlike the Rockettes who have strict height requirements (5'6" to 5'10.5"), the DCC welcomes the height challenged like myself (4'11") to the statuesque. What they do care about is that you look well-proportioned. While they say they have no weight demands, looking proportioned in your rehearsal dancewear—not to mention the DCC uniform—requires a somewhat lean body.

★ Just like the US military, you need to be at least eighteen years old when you walk into the auditions. And since they check out applicants before you show up, don't even think of trying to use a fake ID.

★ There's not much to remember about your tryout attire. Because there's not much to wear. All you wear is an athletic bra, short shorts, skin-tones tights, and shoes. Leave the bike shorts and tank tops or camisoles at home. I buy my outfits online. The DCC recommends a site, but there are a lot of places to choose from.

★ Over the years the DCC organization has really honed in on what they are looking for in applicants. Although splits and high kicks are mandatory by the time the season starts, dance technique is only a part of the scrutiny. They want to see energy in the form of enthusiasm and a sparkling personality. They want poise and a fresh, natural personal appearance, not a face plastered with makeup an inch thick or helmet hair. Just make sure your hair doesn't hang in your face. Most of all they want to see confidence.

Chapter 3

Out of the Nest and into the Spotlight

Up until I was around six years old, I was the most stereotypical little Chinese immigrant you could find. I was timid, quiet, and unquestioning. I was a 100 percent good girl. I never thought to challenge anything my parents said. I did not rebel against them in any way at all. It's not that I necessarily wanted to be good. I simply knew no other way to act.

However, as for rebellious *thoughts* . . . well, my mind was a minefield of resistance. In a way I was caught in a cultural war, and at some point I would need to go on the offensive to get where I wanted to go in life. But until then I needed to pick my battles.

For many teenagers, graduating from high school represents leaving your childhood behind. You might not be financially independent yet, but legally and socially you are considered an adult—unless you're a girl with Taiwanese parents. From my mother's perspective, the only thing changing was the school I attended.

I was never given a choice of colleges. My mother made it clear I would enroll at the school closest to home, so in other words: *Texas A&M here I come.* I didn't bother applying anywhere else.

Even though I'd never been allowed to work and my parents didn't make a lot of money, I wasn't worried about paying for college. I'd spent half my senior year filling out grant and scholarship applications, and the effort paid off. It was amazing just how much assistance I qualified for including a Pell grant and other federal and state grant money; a few low-income scholarships; the Brazos County A&M Club leadership scholarship; and scholarships for students with good grades. It was more than enough to cover my tuition back then because tuition for state schools was affordable for most students.

There was also money for room and board, so I asked my parents' permission to live in the dorm. You can imagine how well that went over. I knew the answer would be no; it was more a gentle reminder that I wasn't going to live at home forever. So I saved the money I would have spent on a dorm and approached college as if it were my job.

It was important to do well for a number of reasons. First, as an immigrant I felt a deep responsibility to my adopted country, which I love and appreciate. I was thankful for the grants that made my education possible and gave me the chance to succeed in this great country. I never felt that needing grants was anything to be ashamed of because I knew I was going to repay the generosity by becoming a successful, contributing member of my community.

Also, your medical future all depends on your grades. I don't mean just getting into med school; your specialty is decided by what kind of grades you make. People don't usually tell you that. You can't just decide: *Oh, I want to be a surgeon.* You better have really high grades if you want to make your living in an operating room. On the other hand, anyone can be an internist.

For example, there are about 146 entry-level residency spots for neurosurgery and 183 for plastic surgery compared to more than 6,500 in internal medicine. Whenever you'd hear someone say: *Oh,*

I decided not to do surgery, more often than not it was because their grades didn't make the cut.

On the other hand, some specialties are very competitive not because they necessarily require the best skills, but because they provide a nice lifestyle: good hours, good pay, and not being on call much. This includes specialties like pediatrics.

One specialty there is a lot of demand for is pathology, but it's considered very low on the totem pole because few people want to be stuck in a morgue with dead people, and it's stinky. But you'd pretty much have your pick of jobs because there are shortages nationwide.

You don't have to declare your specialty until your third or fourth year so I just concentrated on acing my undergrad years. One casualty of focusing all my time and energy on classwork was running. Fitness in general stopped being a part of my life, and it would be many years before I found my way back to it. You often hear about student-athletes, but in my experience most of the student-athletes on the dean's list are rarely pre-med. I met one girl in pre-med who got a scholarship because she was on the track team, but after one semester she had to quit the team. She said it had to be one or the other.

During my college years, I was getting increasingly frustrated over my lack of freedom—even with what I wanted to eat. From the time I started college, my mother insisted I meet her every evening at 7:00 p.m. in one of the university's parking lots. My college days went late, but I was not allowed to eat dinner on campus. Instead, I'd trudge to a parking lot and have dinner sitting in the passenger seat of her car. It might have technically been dinner, but calling it food was being generous. Every night it was exactly the same: a bowl of beef tips, green beans, and white rice drizzled with grease from cooking the meat. Then she would have me do whatever paperwork she needed done.

That was my college life. I lived at home, and my roommate was my grade school sister who I shared a bed with.

One day leaving the house I told my mother she didn't need to bring anything for me to eat that night because I had too many things to do on campus. And I did. Just not academic things. I had joined the Opera and Performing Arts Society (OPAS) at school, and if you volunteered as an usher you could hear the concerts for free. So that night instead of eating in the car, I enjoyed an à la carte dinner in the Memorial Student Center for $3.25. Then I went off to usher with my fellow volunteers. It was the best evening of my college life up to that point, until my mother picked me up at 10:30 p.m. at the same parking lot where I had my nightly meal.

She demanded to know what I had eaten for dinner. I know I should have claimed I'd been too busy studying to eat, but a little of that rebelliousness I had buried for so long bubbled to the surface, so I responded, "Chicken, two vegetables, and a roll ... all for just $3.25."

She was furious; her face flushed red, and she berated me all the way home. The short five-minute drive felt interminable. You would have thought I'd confessed to knocking over the local convenience store for a couple of Big Bites. She demanded I not spend money on food again. It wasn't logical, so I concluded she simply wanted me at her beck and call. To keep the peace, I went back to meeting her at 7:00 p.m. and swallowing her tasteless concoction, along with my resentment.

For the next two years my life revolved around my studies. After my sophomore year, I lived in Houston for six weeks to do a pre-med clerkship. My mother let me attend the program after I persuaded her that it would improve my chances of getting into medical school.

Even though I was physically away, I was still responsible for running my parents' household. My mother gave me letters to write, mail to answer, and other paperwork tasks. I also had to call various companies' customer service to dispute charges, set terms of agreement, request extensions, and so on. My father added his own pile of bookkeeping.

Every time I talked to my mother that summer she reiterated sternly that the moment my internship was done, she needed me back there immediately. I heard her, but I was listening to my own voices seeking to break some chains. I don't think it was a conscious decision, but I knew it was time for a change. It was time for me to go from my parents' home. All I needed was a window of opportunity. I had no idea what form it would take; I just had to be ready for anything.

The opportunity presented itself in January 1986. I was a nineteen-year-old junior in college. I didn't have a boyfriend and wasn't dating. I was too busy applying to medical schools to lament my nonexistent social life. Then I met a fellow medical student while I was touring the University of Texas Health Science Center School of Medicine in San Antonio (UTHSCSA). He was one of the many people I met when I was taken on tour. I asked what kind of doctor he wanted to be. He said surgeon, so I put a mental asterisk by that.

After I was accepted at UTHSCSA, I called him up and shared my good news. I also mentioned I was in San Antonio staying with my friend Sharon. He suggested we go out to dinner. It was very informal, not really a date. I said yes.

After we ate it was still early, so he asked if I wanted to go see a movie. I had rarely seen any films up to that point in my life, and I was really curious, so I was like: *Oh, yeah. Let's go.* We saw *Out of Africa.*

After the movie we were walking outside, and he just said, "Let's get married."

I thought for a moment, calculating, and said, "I could only do it July 19 or 26. That gives me a cushion in case something happens on the nineteenth."

I *always* choose an earlier date in case some crisis happens. I've been programmed to expect calamity thanks to all the ER runs and abrupt moves cross country. But I digress.

He agreed. We were getting married.

My friend Kay picked me up when I got back, and on the drive home I told her I was getting married.

"Married?" She looked at me. "Don't you need a boyfriend first? You're not even dating anyone."

My mother's reaction when I told her—a week later—was even more surprised . . . bordering on the hysterical. After she calmed down, our short conversation exchange went something like this:

"Who is he?"

"A medical student. I found him in San Antonio."

"When do I get to meet him?"

"I'm not sure. I don't have time right now."

"Why don't you get engaged first?"

"Okay, I'll fit it in during June, and then we'll still get married in July."

Our schools were not close together, so we didn't see each other much during that time. I found the apartment long distance and ordered the invitations and everything else via mail order.

About a month before the wedding date, my mother started having a nervous breakdown. One day I walked in, and she was just sitting there crying, saying, "What am I gonna do? What am I gonna do without you? What am I gonna do now that you're getting married?"

And I'm thinking: *Oh my gosh, so that's what she's upset about.* I realized then her refusal to let me have any kind of social life to speak of in high school or college wasn't keeping the reins of her teenage girl tight because she was worried about me losing my virginity and setting off on my own version of *Rumspringa*. It was about her. What I heard in her tears was: *I need to have my taskmaster. I don't have a hand without her. I don't have a mouth without my daughter. My daughter is my everything.* It was like I was her conduit to her American world. She had become totally dependent and felt she didn't have anyone.

Just because I understood didn't mean I thought it was healthy. It wasn't. My mother had been gainfully employed for most of my life, so clearly she could function when we weren't together. It was just easier to dump the household responsibilities on me. Same with my father although he did not respond with tears at the news of my upcoming nuptials. He exuded displeasure. If you ever see the picture of my father's face while he's walking me down the aisle, it says everything.

In keeping with Chinese tradition, we were married at the groom's home, which was in California. For me, it was a bit like having an out-of-body experience, which I wrote about in my memoir, *Grown-Up Child.*

July 19, 1986. Today is my wedding day. I'm twenty years old, surrounded by dozens of people I've never met. What a day: The Christian ceremony, the Chinese reception, and my two different, floor-length gowns—one lacy white, the other a Chinese style design with a high-neck collar in red, the standard color for good fortune. My father's sad, grim, angry face, mourning all the way down the aisle. My mother's sheer panic. My fiancé's parents in opposition to the whole thing. My brother and sister, confused, startled, trying to figure out what's going on.

There are English-speaking Caucasian people, and Taiwanese people who don't speak English. And there are four furiously mad parents, silently kicking and screaming. His parents are wondering how a 26-year-old medical student can decide to marry a young girl he's just met; a girl they don't even know. *What kind of vixen is this girl?*

My husband and I started our lives together with four seething parents because none of them got to meet their respective child's future spouse until a day before the wedding. But they all had to carry on politely in front of all the guests.

A postscript about my mom. In the end, she still saved paperwork for me. Even after I was married and in medical school, whenever I came home there'd be a pile of documents for me to go through. It had turned into a ritual to stay connected.

My husband and I eventually ended up in the same city as medical students at the UTHSCSA. We later lived in California where I started my psychiatric residency at Cedar Sinai in Los Angeles while he attended UCLA as a neurology resident. Then we came back to Texas where I finished my residency, and we settled in Dallas. Eventually we had two sons, and between being a wife, mother, and physician, life was busy doing things mostly for other people, not myself.

I never thought: *Oh my God, I really need to get into the gym and get fit. I really need to start working out.* Remember, my parents discouraged me from working out. They believed I'd become masculine or something. Honestly, it was more a matter of curiosity.

There was a point back in the 1980s when it seemed like gyms were popping up everywhere. When I was in LA, a doctor friend of mine belonged to an expensive private health club in Brentwood that had a restaurant, spa, and valet parking. When we got back to Dallas there were even more gyms because the land was so much cheaper than in LA. So I decided, *Let's see what this is all about* because it was so prevalent. I joined a gym called Premier Club. I'm a very curious person, so I took a lot of different classes and enjoyed it. Plus, the club had a lot of members, so it was a good way to get to know people since I had just moved to the city.

I started going to the gym regularly on the weekend. I didn't have time during the week. In late 1998, my boys were in about first and third grade. I'd get up around 5:30 every morning to get myself and the kids ready for the day. I'd usually drop them off at the school's daycare by 7:30, go to work, then pick them up after work, take them home, feed them, put them to bed, and then start all over again the next morning.

I didn't work on weekends, so I could spend time at the gym because it had a daycare center where I could put the kids while I took my classes. It was really neat, and my kids loved it because they had all these gadgets. I actually liked the gym daycare better than the school daycare they went to. And my kids started making their own little friends there too. The club got all of us out on the weekend. Staying in a small apartment all day with two young children would drive you—and them—crazy. So we had a nice regular routine going.

One day in January 1999 the step class instructor, Kim, walked up to me.

"Hey, I got this letter from the Dallas Cowboys Cheerleaders organization. They're recruiting for new people."

Let me stop here and explain that I'm a bit of a dichotomy. While I may have been born in Taiwan and do not have big Texas hair and barely stand five feet tall and a hundred pounds carrying luggage, I sound as if my Texas roots go back to the Republic. My accent is completely down home country, so people assume I grew up immersed in Texas culture, which of course includes barbecue, tailgating, and football.

So imagine the expression on Kim's face when she asked, "You know the Dallas Cowboys, right?" and I looked at her as if I'd suddenly gone aphasic.

I finally said, "Yeah ... kind of ... not really."

After her shock subsided, she showed me the letter, and the first thing I saw was the blue and pink star at the top. The whole presentation was so pretty. I remember reading, *The Dallas Cowboys Cheerleaders: America's Sweethearts* and something about high-kicks, fan-kicks, the splits, and a routine. It turned out Kim was a former Cowboys cheerleader and the organization was putting the call out for that year's auditions, which were then in April.

Now, as I've explained, I was kept so insulated in high school that even had I been aware that you could try out for cheerleading, I wouldn't have been interested. I didn't have the time, and I wouldn't have known what to do. But that was then. Once again I sensed a window of opportunity opening.

"Kim, how do I try out? I don't know anything about that kind of stuff."

She explained the Dallas Cowboys Cheerleaders held preparation classes on Wednesday nights at the enormous Dallas Cowboys Valley Ranch training facility. Back then it was sparkling new, and I was mesmerized. It was beautiful and had all these life-sized pictures of gorgeous, glamourous women on the wall. I thought: *My goodness, what is this?* I was just so impressed by the whole presentation and atmosphere.

I walked into an area called the dance academy and took the class. My childhood friend Janine's best efforts notwithstanding, I didn't know how to dance and knew going in I'd be a couple of steps behind and playing catch up to everyone else. I'm sure by the time I left my joints and muscles were in a state of shock, but I was on such a high just from being in that environment. I wondered: *Could I be one of those ladies on the wall too?*

Then I thought about the kicks and other moves I needed to learn. So I went back to Kim and told her I was going to do the tryouts then asked if I could hire her. I offered to pay her thirty dollars for thirty minutes every Saturday to tutor me and help me get a routine together incorporating the moves they were teaching at the prep classes because obviously that's what they wanted to see at the audition. She agreed.

Well, when we got started, I had no idea what dancers did. During that first session, I literally couldn't kick higher than knee level. Considering I needed to get those legs up past waist level and have that knee whack my nose—it's got to go boom and come on down—it was clear I had a lot of work to do.

My body was not amused. I was in pain every day, but I was determined to make that first audition and had three and a half months to get ready. On Wednesdays I'd get a babysitter for the kids so I could attend the prep class. I worked hard, and when the audition came around in April 1999, I was ready.

One night while I was at the prep class, a TV news reporter from WB33 (now CW33) interviewed me about trying out and told me it would air as a feature story on the nine o'clock evening news. The hook then was that I was a doctor trying out for the Dallas Cowboys Cheerleaders. I flashed back to when I was a little girl and the local paper ran my photo on the front page. I experienced the same sensation of validation as I had thirty years earlier. And I thought: *I kind of like this being in the limelight.* I was also proud of just the physical accomplishment of going from an eleven-year-old who couldn't do a chin hold to a woman trying out for Dallas Cowboys Cheerleaders.

You know, my parents didn't always have a harmonious relationship, but on this point they were in solid agreement: you have to work hard. There's no such thing as luck. Talent is secondary; work is primary. I have applied that truism to every facet of my life, including participating in a cheerleading tryout.

My philosophy is definitely not to sit around wishing and hoping. If you don't put in the time, it's just not going to happen. People who are more successful have usually put in more time than you have. Instead of strategizing just work at it, and you'll figure out how to do it better and faster. But sometimes all that determination takes you in some unexpected directions, which is what happened in the wake of my quixotic DCC quest.

DALLAS, March 31, 2003 /PRNewswire/ -- It's one thing to achieve one's dream in life. It is quite another to achieve a dream and then set about making a totally different but equally ambitious dream come true.

That is just what Chiufang Hwang, MD is doing. The Dallas-based doctor and mother is pursuing her dream of becoming one of the few nationally recognized Asian-American models. Having achieved her career goal as a doctor, she was presented with the chance to pursue her long-held modeling and acting dream.

The 5'1" mother of two first realized that her dream could become a reality when she tried out for the Dallas Cowboys Cheerleaders in 2002. She had previously appeared in an infomercial for the Chuck Norris Total Gym, which aired throughout the 2001 year and opened the door to the cheerleader tryouts. It was at the tryouts that Chiufang was discovered by TransContinental Talent (TCTalent).

"I realized that as a doctor and a psychiatrist I was limited," says Chiufang. "I see a lack of role models for Asian-Americans and I want to give back to the community. When I got recruited by TCT and then signed on by Dallas-based Horne Agency, I realized it was a once-in-a-lifetime opportunity, and I better grab it quick."

Chiufang is currently one of D Magazine's finalists for Most Beautiful in Dallas, and she travels to Orlando at the end of March to participate in the TCTalent Fashion Rock modeling competition. Chiufang is also TCTalent's model of the month for March.

Adds Chiufang, "As a nationally recognized personality, I will be able to achieve so much more for Asian-Americans and the wider community as a whole."

Okay, no, I didn't hang up my medical license in exchange for a modeling career; yes, I may have fudged just a bit on my height; and maybe I downplayed my extracurricular pursuits to my family even though I was having the time of my life.

Past Cheerleaders Megan Fox and Natalie Woods Reminisce[19]

For the women who are part of the team, is this a steppingstone onto something else, or is this the pinnacle of your career?

Megan Fox: For those us of, as performers—I mean, really, most of us have danced or done some type of cheerleading our entire lives, so this is really that bar that we've really worked so hard to reach. I really think that this is a dream come true. And for some of us it will be the end of our performing careers; but for others, we'll go on to teach, hopefully, and continue to be involved in the dance and performance world. But really, this is just the icing on the cake for most of us.

Natalie Woods: I agree with Megan; it was the icing on the cake. I've been very blessed. I have a career. I've been a reporter for *ABC News Live*. And for me ... I moved to Dallas, and I knew that they had the cheerleaders. I thought: *Hmm, maybe I can give that a shot. Maybe I'll make it past preliminaries.* And then all of a sudden I made it into training camp and boy, the entire process that we went through—it was a rude awakening.

What's the continuing appeal of being a part of this squad?

Natalie Woods: I grew up near Houston, and I wasn't actually a Dallas Cowboys fan. I was a Houston Oilers fan, but I was always a Dallas Cowboys Cheerleader fan because of the history, the pride. I also saw the movie, and I knew that I wanted to be a part of that, and I wanted to don that uniform.

Megan Fox: And we're an organization that's very involved, I believe both nationally and internationally. I think there's that very large fan base, not just for the Cowboys, but for the cheerleaders as well.

Has being on TV in *Making the Team* changed the way auditions are conducted?

Megan Fox: I auditioned before this television process ever came around, and I can vouch for the fact that it is identical to what I did my first year before the television show was ever introduced. It's been an adjustment, I think, for those of us that have come back and done it again, but I can definitely vouch that it's the same process.

Natalie Woods: I have one more comment. I actually tried out last year as well. I was one of the very last cut. It hurt to get cut, but the one thing that I appreciated was their honesty. I think some people forget that this is a professional organization and honesty is expected because we are paid, and we are recognized as a part of the Dallas Cowboys organization. So anything less than honesty in the way they handle things would have been disappointing for me.

Chapter 4

Ready for My Close-Up

The morning after the WB33 feature story on me came out, I was rushing to get the kids to school. I had a busy day scheduled and needed to drop the kids off the minute the school opened, so I got there early, around 6:45. The doors open, I take my kids in, then turn around to leave when the principal comes running after me and calls out. Of course my thoughts immediately go to the dark place. *Oh my God, did the school shut down? Is there a fire?*

The principal catches up to me and says, "Hey, I saw you on the TV news last night, right?"

"Yes, that was me."

"I told my wife that was one of our parents, and she didn't believe me." He was just so excited, and of course I loved the attention.

That evening when the kids came home, my eldest said, "Hey, Mom, Brandon's mom said that you're a Dallas Cowboys Cheerleader."

Whoa, offspring. I said, "Let me set this straight; I'm just trying out for that. For fun. I'm not one. Yet."

"Okay, that's kind of cool."

After that they got used to it, and over the years I took them with me to various DCC events like calendar signings. And one time I took my husband to a production the cheerleaders put on called the *Friends and Family Show*—I called it an end-of-the-year recital— which he seemed to enjoy.

While he eventually became aware that I was attending the tryouts, back in 1999 I hadn't mentioned it. When you're with someone you learn their style, and it really wasn't something he would have wholeheartedly supported. From what I've seen, few men are. Over the years I've gotten to know of lot of the ladies who try out or have made the team. Those who are married admit their husbands ask: *Do you really have to do that again this year?* because it is so incredibly time consuming. The game might be just a few hours a week, but rehearsal pretty much becomes their life. At the auditions they warn aspiring cheerleaders about the time commitment involved for those selected to attend the training camp.

After the audition process whittles the team down from hundreds of aspirants to around forty-five ladies, those selected will spend the next two months or so rehearsing almost every night for at least four hours, as Kelli and Judy work to get them prepared. It takes me months to perfect one short routine; at camp they have to learn more than fifty song-and-dance numbers. And if you miss a rehearsal before a home game during the season—for any reason—you don't get to work that game. And if you accumulate two unexcused absences before a game performance, you can be permanently cut.

And I thought my mother was tough. But that's the price for striving to perfection.

Back in 1999, my husband—who I call Doc—knew I was into fitness but not that I was training to try out for the Dallas Cowboys Cheerleaders team. The day after the TV station ran the feature on me, Doc was at the hospital, and someone mentioned to him they'd seen on the news where a Dr. Hwang who looked just like his wife was trying out to be a Cowboys cheerleader. Now, Huang is a common Taiwanese name so Doc shrugged it off, but the other physician was adamant it was me. So when he came home he asked me. I acknowledged it was me, that I was taking special fitness classes that many of the cheerleaders took, and that I assumed they'd singled me out because not many Chinese women attended the classes.

Like me, Doc wasn't into the Texas sports culture. He knew who the Cowboys were, but he didn't come to the United States until he was seventeen, so sports like football weren't part of his universe. He didn't understand what a big cultural deal the Dallas Cowboys Cheerleaders were. To him, what I was doing wasn't all that different from me working out at the gym on weekends. And as long as it didn't interfere with my family and professional responsibilities, he didn't care. So I just went about my business and kept training with Kim and going to prep classes. And even though I had aches and pains everywhere, I never let on.

There were years here and there when I didn't make it to tryouts, but I always went to the prep classes and kept working to become a better dancer. I got involved with the tryouts when I was thirty-four and like they say, it's never too late to start. My attitude was: *Who knows?* I just wanted to see how much better I could get. And in the process, the ideal of limitless possibilities made me feel like a teenage girl. There's something about me that just loves being on stage. That loves the attention. So I kept going to auditions, which is how I ended up on late night TV in an infomercial.

Reps from Transcontinental Talent came to the auditions in 2003 scouting for new faces. They took my photo and pitched me to the Horne Agency, which sent me auditions for various work. I did not consider it modeling in the typical sense of the word. I ended up appearing in some commercials, a print ad for a mattress firm, and training videos for IBM.

I was with the Horne Agency for about four years. It was just something that happened. I am very comfortable in front of the camera, and it gave me the opportunity to learn something about the industry. It was mostly on the weekends, and I didn't make a big deal out of it. Again, my family didn't know when I went to auditions; they only knew if a commercial or print ad came out when I showed it to them. For example, I was one of eight people cast for the debut Match. com commercial. My husband and sons knew about that one, and it aired on E Channel for several years. I also did a couple Total Gym infomercials with Chuck Norris and Christie Brinkley that ran all the time. I was the one doing the sit-ups. Had I not kept auditioning for the DCC, I would have never been scouted by the talent agency and would have never gotten to experience commercial work. It was fun and made me feel good about myself. I enjoyed exploring the different sides of my personality. I spent most of my life doing things for others; this was one area where I was doing it just for me.

And to be honest, I also saw auditioning as a kind of competition. I was competing to see who would ultimately get picked. I saw it as a challenge to see just how many call backs I could get. I would study each casting director to see what they were looking for and then prep myself to meet that angle to get selected. One thing I realized early on is that they want you prepped, ready to go, so I always arrived early. Not long after that, the different agencies started requesting me. I also very much enjoyed the regimen of getting down to the weight and size the agency casted you for.

Not surprisingly, my parents were very against all of it once they found out, which wasn't until 2015. I showed them a newspaper article about me auditioning for the DCC. and my mother's first comment was about the photo they used.

"Did you realize your navel is showing?"

My mother then wanted to know how much the newspaper had paid me for the article. I explained you don't get paid for newspaper articles. She pointed out the tabloids paid. How she knew about tabloids intrigued me, but I didn't go there.

After he finished reading the article my dad asked, "What's the point of this?"

They simply don't understand what I'm getting out of it. To them

I'm squandering my time. They look down on it as … unseemly. As if I was lowering myself. Doing something just for the fun of it and to improve your self-esteem is not something promoted in the Chinese culture. They considered both my involvement and the final product frivolous. It's never surprised me that I've only ever seen a handful of Asian ladies trying out at the DCC auditions. There are a couple of professional dancers who came from Japan, but I don't recall seeing first generation Chinese-Americans trying out. There are just so many cultural issues for old school immigrants like my parents.

But I discovered over the years that negativity can come from anywhere. When I first started in 1999, after the news piece came out, I had a physician friend email me: *How can you do something that lowers women? You're a professional, we worked all our lives to get where we are, and this is just so downgrading, treating women as property …* and all this other stuff.

There was also some professional jealousy. The UTHSCSA newsletter *The Mission,* did an article on me titled "Keeping Up with Dr. Huang."

If you were looking for Chiufang H. Hwang, M.D., in 1992, you probably would have found her buried beneath a stack of books.

"I was a library worm back then," Dr. Hwang said.

If you were looking for her today, you'd want to pick up the *Dallas Morning News* or flip through a few channels on your television set.

The 1992 School of Medicine graduate is a psychiatrist, a wife, a mother of two, a special events planner, a public relations specialist, a commercial/print model and a featured guest in television commercials. To say she's "on the go" is a bit of an understatement.

Dr. Hwang lives in Dallas, where she's had the opportunity to work as a social conduit and events planner for Bill Blass Outerwear, an internationally recognized fashion label. She also has done public relations for Saks Fifth Avenue and currently is working with Haldane, an executive career management firm, and the Hedge Funds Care/Mike Modano Foundation.

You might also find her pulling stomach crunches with Chuck Norris and Christie Brinkley—she did the abdomen portion of the Total Gym infomercial. If you didn't catch the commercials, perhaps you spotted her on the news. KDAF, KTVT, and KXAS—the Warner Brothers, CBS, and NBC stations in Dallas/Fort Worth—all featured Dr. Hwang in their newscasts. IBM Global used her in a computer commercial.

Exhausted? Not Dr. Hwang. "This stems from my early childhood. Because English was not the first language for my parents, I viewed every document, such as apartment leases and job applications, that went through the household," Dr. Hwang said. "Functioning as a child-parent made me realize that opportunities in life only happen once, and when they do, I go at it 150 percent."

Dr. Hwang completed her psychiatry residency at Cedars-Sinai Medical Center in Los Angeles and a fellowship in child and adolescent psychiatry at the UT Southwestern Medical Center at Dallas.

After the article was published, a male physician told me, "Hey, my wife looked at your article, and she just made some very nasty comments."

I told him it was okay; I was used to it. The more notoriety I've gotten, whether professionally or because of the DCC, the more negativity I've gotten from certain women. It's interesting. And it's not necessarily overt hostility; it's subtler, more sarcastic. *Don't you have something better to do in your free time?* I'm not sure how what I do affects them. I just learned that you can't count on support from others. You have to believe in yourself, and you have to shut out all the negativity. They want to put me in a box. But just because I make time for myself to train for the DCC or enjoy doing interviews about my life doesn't mean I shirk my familial or professional duties. I openly admit I'm a classic Type A personality and thrive on a full appointment book.

I've always been a compulsive reader, even though I've always suspected I had a reading disability because I read very slowly. But I love, love, love to read and have an insatiable appetite for knowledge. I'm passionate about keeping up with the latest in medicine. I religiously read every issue of the *New England Journal of Medicine* and have for years.

Besides professional journals, I want to know anything about everything. I read news, biographies, trashy novels—anything. I just have to read the *New York Times,* the *Dallas Morning News,* and the *Wall Street Journal.* When I travel, I have to buy the local newspaper because I want to know what's happening in that town. It's so neurotic it drives me crazy. I'll read tabloids and stuff like the *National Enquirer, People* magazine.

I still work full time at the clinic I manage. I get there about 8:15 a.m. or so, depending on traffic. And then I have to make sure the staff is in, both the front desk staff and the medical staff. You learn when people are trying to get off work, and I'm pretty stern about that. When an employee calls in saying they don't feel well, I'll say, "I'm giving you two hours to go to urgent care, get me a note, and then get back here."

They usually skip the clinic and just show up. That's something I deal with constantly: *Who's going to clock in today, who's not?* I also have to deal with vendors, like the time the cable company wouldn't release my phone line after we switched carriers. After I make sure everybody comes in, I do a little staff meeting and dole out the charts because if you don't assign them, the charts just sit there and nobody goes through them. And then in those charts you have to call patients. Or the patients call you. And there are pharmacies to confer with. I tell you what: a clinic does not run by itself.

Doc and I founded Parent Partners for those whose kids are first year medical students—referred to as MS1—and no, it's not a coincidence that our son is now a medical student at our alma mater. Even though the medical school's in San Antonio, there were enough parents in Dallas to form a group. I also started the Dallas chapter for our alumni association and have been very involved in it including serving on the board and putting on our annual events.

But one of my favorite things is giving commencement speeches, like this one from May 2016 at the UTHSCSA School of Medicine.

May I be the first fellow alum to address you as *doctor*.

It was nearly a quarter century ago that I sat in those seats on a day like this. I was very proud, as you all should be right now. Finally, I was receiving that Doctor of Medicine degree and that hard-earned diploma. For me this ceremony was especially significant because up until that day, I only had a high school diploma. I started school here after three years of undergraduate studies.

You've worn your white coats since your first semester. Today, you'll put away your waist-length white coats because your new ones will extend all the way down below your knees. That's a mark of growth!

And that long white coat symbolizes the power of knowledge you've acquired here with the responsibility to go out into this world and heal people, in whichever specialty you choose.

At such a moment, it's natural to feel invincible. From my point of view as a child and adolescent psychiatrist, I've seen many teenagers wearing these cloaks of invincibility. They're young and strong, and they're sure they can do just about anything and not get harmed.

Likewise, medical education gives us doctors the enormous power to heal people, our patients. But what I realized during my career is that no matter how much knowledge you've gained or how skillful your hands—even if you become the best surgeon—you just can't escape being human. We doctors are not machines. We might seem and feel superhuman at times, but we are more human than not.

Sadly, doctors often fail to take care of their own bodies and then try to heal others. The truth is that we can succumb to the same diseases and illnesses as our patients, and we might even end up worse than those we treat.

For me, it happened early on and caught me by surprise. During my fellowship I went to the university clinic one afternoon because my eyes were getting itchy and inflamed, which I attributed to allergies. I was first seen by the resident, then fellow, then when the faculty attending physician examined me even more thoroughly I sensed from his body language that this was more serious. I was diagnosed with glaucoma and treatment started immediately.

I thought this was a disease that old people get. I was only twenty-nine years old.

A few years ago, my knuckles and fingers began to swell, and then I couldn't remove my ring when I was washing my hands. There was swelling in my other joints as well. On a blood draw, we found elevated levels of anti-CCP (a specific marker), positive rheumatoid factor, and elevated sed rate.[1] Since the onset had been slow and once again insidious, I didn't know I had rheumatoid arthritis.

So two chronic illnesses, no cure for either, but with daily medications for treatment, my symptoms have not worsened.

What saddens me the most is that some of my classmates with whom I shared lecture halls and gross anatomy lab, those who sat next to me during all these classes, have died before their time. What a terrible shame to spend all these years in

---

[1] A sedimentation rate, also called a sed rate, is a blood test which detects nonspecific inflammation. It is typically ordered when a doctor suspects arthritis.

medical school, learning about our bodies, and then we don't even take care of our own bodies.

Doctors, we are not invincible. We must take the time to take care of ourselves because you can't effectively take care of others if you neglect yourself.

Still, there are times when physical treatment doesn't solve the ailment. Through the years I have come across illnesses that cannot be healed physically. There is no logic to explain why this patient has been afflicted with this terrible disease. My own sister was found to have acute lymphocytic leukemia at age two, had a successful treatment on clinical trials, then died suddenly at age thirteen while I was in medical school.

Human suffering causes our minds to generate feelings of anger, fear, and pain. Regardless of what happens to the body, true healing takes place in the mind, the calming effects of healing our souls. As a physician, wife, mother of two sons and an immigrant, I have always had to overcome adversity. I have found healing through writing, now authoring two autobiographical books and a third book in progress.

You are here to heal, and you are your most important patient. Be vigilant about your own health first. And when you sense you have a problem, embrace it because it will make you a better healer.

My fellow doctors, my message to you: heal thyself first, so you can heal others.

I've also been asked to speak at several white coat ceremonies, which is for when the incoming first-year medical students are presented with their white medical coat. Here's the speech I gave in July 2015. It was special because my son was in that group of 220 medical students.

Thank you for inviting me to be part of this special day. It's an honor to be here with all of you.

My, what a fine-looking group of young men and women. And smart, too! Well, you can't beat that combination! Welcome, entering medical class of 2019.

It was not so long ago that I sat in those same seats on a day like this. Well, actually, it was almost three decades ago. Among those sitting with you right now, someone will become your best friend. Someone else might become your maid of honor, best man, or maybe even your husband or wife. Your future practice partner might be sitting near you today.

For me, I came here to get my MD. Well, that happened. Unexpectedly, I also ended up getting my Mrs.—to another medical student at this school. And sometime after that, a baby, too. Yes, all right here!

The truth is things don't always go as planned. I had set my sights on becoming an ER doctor because I was drawn to the drama and intensity, the excitement.

You see, my family made lots of trips to the emergency room (much like university hospital & the Robert B. Green), and since my parents didn't speak English well, I was the family spokesperson. *My little brother almost sliced off his finger,* I would say to the triage nurse. *My baby sister has a fever.*

One night when my baby sister was two and a half, she started convulsing so we rushed to the ER. That night she was diagnosed with acute lymphocytic leukemia.

Doctors told us that she couldn't be cured, could only prolong her life. Back in the 70s, there were no protocols for treating leukemia. So my little sister went through clinical trials, not knowing if these treatments would work, cocktail mixture of chemo and radiation, would save her life or would kill her.

I went into the exam rooms and watched her go through these traumatic procedures—painful bone marrow aspirations with a huge metal tube stuck into her hip.

And that's when I decided to become a doctor and help

people. I was eleven years old. So actually, my sister inspired me to become a doctor.

During my second year of school here, I got a phone call from my brother who found her dead. She was thirteen years old. My little sister had died in her sleep.

I was in shock and couldn't continue emotionally. When life takes a sad, unexpected turn, it doesn't matter how smart you are, or how caring. These cruel forces threw me off my feet. My thoughts were frozen and I kept thinking back to my sister's body. Every time I heard an ambulance, I thought of her. I couldn't read or concentrate. Every time I saw a cadaver, I thought I saw my sister.

The same person who propelled me to go into medicine was the same figure who was holding me back—I couldn't continue because my grief was so overwhelming.

The Associate Dean for Student Affairs at the time granted me a leave of absence. And that was a pivotal moment in my life: I decided to become a psychiatrist. Having experienced first-hand someone dying, the searing pain of my sister dying so suddenly, I realized that psychiatry was my calling. And the truth was that I had an edge over those who'd never experienced something so painful.

I shared my personal story with you because you've chosen a challenging route. You never know what might happen along the way or if something goes wrong, so ask for help. Luckily, you have chosen a remarkable medical school.

The support of this school helped me through the death of the person who inspired me to go into medicine. So, if you're not at the top of your class, don't worry about it. After all, only one person can be at the top of this class.

The unpredictable nature of life means that cruel forces can push you off your path unexpectedly. If that ever happens to you, don't, don't, please don't give up.

Remember, you're not alone in this great endeavor. Thank you, and my best wishes to all.

I was surprised by the reaction to that speech. Several people were moved to tears. People lined up to shake my hand. I felt like I had delivered the world's best Oscar speech. I also felt like I had stolen the dean's thunder. He got over it and asked me to speak again at the next ceremony, but it won't be as personal because my son won't be in the audience listening.

As part of my work with the alumni association, I also have to solicit support from graduating doctors. I call it my sales pitch.

It was nearly a quarter century ago, I sat in those seats on a day like this. Getting that hard-earned Doctor of Medicine degree symbolized the knowledge that I acquired and the responsibility to uphold professional standards of medicine. Because I had spent very crucial years here, I wanted to give back to the school and to the people here. These people became my family because they made my journey a success.

Today, I personally invite you to join me and give back to our alma mater. How? Whatever town you live in, you can form a local chapter. I started the Dallas chapter six years ago. We have grown together to the point that these are now some of my closest friends.

Reinvest in the future generations of our medical students by starting a class scholarship and contribute financially. We need money to grow.

How about mentoring to our medical students? Every August we host a residency roundup. And wherever you are living, you can host a fourth-year medical student who is interviewing for residency, through our HOST program.

In order to continue growing, we need, as a team, to explore ways to help our medical school and our medical community. Join me by serving on the board.

A few months from now, come back here for a quick weekend. Every October, we host our annual reunion weekend. It's like a family reunion. I have met some new friends at these reunions, because they understand what I have gone through here. We also offer support; that's our Parent Partners program.

My fellow doctors, on behalf of the School of Medicine Alumni Association, please join me by giving back to our school. And stay connected to our family.

The point I'm making is that in no way has my involvement with the DCC tryouts negatively impacted my responsibilities; on the contrary, it's complemented my life. It fills in the blanks I didn't realize were missing. And it is also a statement of defiance against letting rheumatoid arthritis keep me from pursuing my goals.

CMT's vice president of development Melanie Moreau, and Kelli Finglass discuss *Making the Team* [20, 21]

The *Dallas Cowboys Cheerleaders: Making the Team* is a docuseries that follows a group of hopefuls as they endure rigorous auditions, training camp, and endless rehearsals for a chance to become part of the Dallas Cowboys Cheerleaders squad.

How grueling is the practice schedule in training camp?

Moreau: The girls rehearse five nights a week. Rehearsal starts at 7:00 and runs until 11:00, but many get to rehearsal at 5:30 because they are expected to learn fifty dances in eight weeks. The pace of learning is very fast. They practically learn a new dance every night and are expected to come back the next day ready to perform it.

During the age of staged reality TV, many people may not realize how real the show is, that these women are actually competing.

Why was that always important to demonstrate?

Moreau: From day one we wanted to stay true to the authentic process these girls go through to make the team because we wanted our viewers to see the process for what it really is: incredibly challenging, life-changing, and intimidating. It is a real competition, and yet the girls are all super supportive of each other. You can feel a true sense of camaraderie. If someone is struggling they usually buddy up and help one another. They are cheerleaders for each other.

Has there been anything special done to accommodate the television production? Do you do things differently in any way—add things, subtract things—that you haven't done before?

> **Finglass:** Not really. The audition process that the television series focuses on is actually the same audition process I went through in the '80s and started in the '70s. The lines are the same. The applications are the same. The dance evaluation, learning choreography, executing in front of judges, panel interviews with our judges ... all of that is the same. And that's because Judy and I are truly going through our day-to-day business of an audition process. And for television or anything else, I wouldn't compromise that or adjust that. At the end of the day, we're looking to pick the best thirty-six members of our team. Judy and I had to get used to having microphones, belt packs, lights—you know, the production element. That's new for us because we didn't have that before. But the integrity of the audition and just the logistics of the operation and all of that has definitely remained the same.

So the way the elimination is presented and the way the people are accepted, that's exactly as it was before TV?

> **Finglass:** It is. We've always taken forty-five, give or take a few, into training camp. We've always invited more into training camp than actually make the full squad of thirty-six. We always have public and candid comments in rehearsals because it's the nature of a rehearsal. But then we've also had private conversations in my office or in the locker room. You know, when it comes down to that final hour and you're letting someone go, the only thing that's different is that it used to be very private, and now it's captured on television. But the conversations, the emotion, the awkwardness ... all

of that is very real. I'm not an actress nor is Judy, and that's quite evident. But we say what we have to, and actually we don't really even notice the cameras.

What surprises you?

Moreau: It's always surprising how many girls come back year after year after being cut the year before. And I believe a lot of people don't realize how hard these girls really work to make the team and accomplish their lifelong dream of being a Dallas Cowboys Cheerleader. The girls work for months training before auditions. They work on their solo presentations and getting their high kicks up to Dallas Cowboys Cheerleaders standards. They have to be in top shape to make it through camp. All the girls say they have never experienced anything as mentally exhausting or physically taxing as training camp. Learning fifty dances in a summer is extremely difficult. Dealing with injury and setbacks can take you off your game, so they need to be mentally tough.

Chapter *5*

Living with Rheumatoid Arthritis

As a kid I learned early that bad things happen when I watched our trailer burn to the ground. I also learned danger can present itself in an instant. It was something that was always on my mind. I recently came across a journal entry from when I was eleven years old.

> You always have to be ready. You never know when it's the next time that you're going to the emergency room. You never know when the next crisis will happen.
>
> You never know when your little brother's going to practically slice his finger off, when your baby sister's going to start convulsing and you leave your food half-eaten, chopsticks poking into their bowls, and you run to the car and speed across town through all the red lights, hoping you make it in time.
>
> You go to sleep thinking that you'd better keep your clothes on and you'd better have your things ready, because how do you know that in the middle of the night, your cozy trailer home is not going to succumb to flames?

> You don't know any of these things. So you always have to
> be ready.

The incident with my brother was really burned into my brain. One Saturday afternoon when he was around three years old he went in the kitchen and got a knife to cut up an orange. Instead he sliced his hand open. I looked up and there's blood everywhere. I had to alert my parents, who were oblivious to what was happening, and have them drive to the emergency room. The upshot is: I grew up being very vigilant and looking out for people. And to this day I'm always prepared for an emergency.

I often travel to go to medical conferences. Once when I got back from a conference in New York City, one of my associates asked what I had done in the evenings. Had I gone to the theatre? Had I walked around and seen the sights? Had I tried any of the wonderful restaurants? I thought a moment and realized my most vivid memory was how every night I carefully laid out my bra, panties, long-sleeved shirt, and a pair of jeans on the hotel room's armoire. I'd set my purse next to it and check to make sure my credit cards and some cash were in it. Only then could I go to sleep.

My associate of course looked at me as if my name was Moonbeam. So I explained that you never know when there's going to be a hotel fire. I might need to jump out of bed, throw on those clothes, grab my purse, and get out of there. That's how I think every day. It might not be my brother cutting his finger or my sister having a seizure, but you just don't know what else could happen.

You can imagine how I was during the four years I lived in Los Angeles when doing part of my residency. I took earthquake preparedness to a whole new level. And every time the buildings would shake I was convinced it was the Big One. After each tremor, I'd think: *What the hell—and I have to be here four years?* So that sense of waiting for the other catastrophic shoe to drop has been programmed into me.

But that worry never included my health. I've never been a hypochondriac. I take care of myself, and I've always been healthy. I often joke I'm too busy to get sick. So the idea I might have a chronic medical condition was the furthest thing from my mind. Until it happened.

It was around 2010 when I started getting some neck and arm pain. Nothing debilitating but enough to be annoying. Like we tend to do, I dismissed it as either soreness from working out or general wear and tear of getting older. But the discomfort was very insidious, very slow. My arm became numb. I couldn't sleep at night because the numbness woke me up.

My first the-sky-is-falling thought, of course, immediately went to the worst-case scenario of a brain tumor. After some reflection I thought it was two neck bones pressing against a nerve or something. So I went to see a neurologist, and he took an MRI of my neck and my back. He was a very meticulous doctor, and after his examination he had a strong suspicion of what was going on.

He told me, "I'm going to run some blood tests for rheumatoid factor."

That was a surprise. Rheumatoid factor, which doctors call RF, is a measurable antibody that can indicate rheumatoid arthritis (RA). Then sure enough, the next day he called and told me my RF factor was so high he wanted to repeat the test to verify. So I met with him again. We repeated the test, and the results were the same so he told me, "You need to go see a rheumatologist."

I was very grateful for the neurologist's thoroughness and for being intuitive enough to consider my problem wasn't neural. I asked him why he had even considered testing my RF.

He said, "Well, you presented with neck pain. The neck is the third most common body part, after hands and feet, to be afflicted with rheumatoid arthritis."

Who knew? Clearly not me.

As usual, once I'm curious about something I go into full

research mode, and I pored over professional medical journals. Even though I'm a physician, my specialty is psychiatry, not joints or autoimmune diseases, so I did a crash course finding out everything I could. I never realized just how many people suffer from arthritis. According to the Arthritis Foundation, a little more than two million Americans are diagnosed with rheumatoid arthritis and three-fourths of them are women. RA generally develops in women between the ages of thirty and sixty. In men, it often occurs later in life. There have also been some cases of young children being afflicted, but that is rare.

The umbrella definition of arthritis is a condition that causes pain and inflammation of joints. There are more than one hundred variants of the condition, which means treatment will vary depending on the particular type an individual has. Two of the best-known types are rheumatoid arthritis and osteoarthritis.

Osteoarthritis is usually a side effect of getting older. It typically manifests in one particular joint and is accompanied by stiffness upon waking and pain in the joint, which increases as the day wears on. Rheumatoid arthritis is a chronic inflammatory disorder that afflicts people in the prime of their life. Its symptoms can include inflammation in the joints, swelling, stiffness, pain, restricted joint movement, and fatigue as well as possible issues with the heart, lungs, or kidneys. RA is an autoimmune disorder, which means your immune system mistakenly attacks your own body's tissues. Because of that, in RA more than a single joint is typically affected.

Unlike the wear-and-tear damage of osteoarthritis, rheumatoid arthritis affects the lining of your joints, causing a painful swelling. Early rheumatoid arthritis tends to affect smaller joints first. Then as the disease progresses, symptoms often spread to the wrists, knees, ankles, elbows, hips and shoulders. In most cases, symptoms occur in the same joints on both sides of your body.

Learning that made me realize I'd been having symptoms for a while and just never thought anything about it. I did have shoulder pain; I've had it all along. And I have hip pain and shoulder pain, but it's just really nonspecific, so it didn't raise any concern. It was more like an annoyance ... until it became an increasingly uncomfortable stiffness.

I was surprised to learn that almost half of those with RA don't experience joint pain symptoms. Instead, it can affect skin, eyes, lungs, heart, kidneys, nerves, and even your bone marrow. The severity of the symptoms varies and sometimes go away completely for a while, before flaring up again. Then the cycle repeats. At its worst, over time, rheumatoid arthritis can cause joints to deform and shift out of place—not something to look forward to. And if that wasn't enough, individuals with RA are up to 50 percent more likely to develop type 2 diabetes. Oh, yea ...

The researchers admit they don't know if the inflammation associated with RA results in insulin resistance, which in turn increases blood sugar levels, or if living a more sedentary lifestyle because of RA pain is what makes you more susceptible.

Also, the steroid medications used to treat arthritis can make it harder to control blood sugar levels. An article I read explained, "When you have a lot of steroids in your body, your body makes glucose because it assumes you're going to need it for some kind of fight-or-flight response. But if you're giving them to someone to control their RA, it can make their sugars higher."[22]

All in all, reading about RA was pretty depressing, especially because doctors still don't know what starts this process. They do think that at least in some cases, there's a genetic component. Not necessarily that a specific gene causes RA; more like you can be genetically more susceptible to certain factors that might trigger the disease. And in thinking back, I remember my grandmother had arthritis so I'm guessing it may run in my family. Researchers also believe RA can have environmental and hormonal causes.

It's easy to feel overwhelmed when confronted with any kind of diagnosis. But I've always been someone who faces challenges head on. Just as I had jumped in with both feet at the cheerleading tryouts, I was going to do whatever it took to keep RA under control.

So when I started seeing my rheumatologist, she ran the whole panel for various autoimmune diseases—lupus, rheumatoid arthritis, Sjogren's syndrome—because there is no single test just for RA. My symptoms could have indicated any number of joint diseases. But after taking my medical history, doing a physical exam, X-rays, and more blood work, the doctor determined I had RA.

By that time, I was so stiff that sometimes it was painful, like after taking a long flight. She said what happens is like a civil war in your body. Your antibodies start attacking your joints or other tissue because it stops recognizing it and thinks it's a foreign invader.

I can tell you there are mornings I wake up feeling like I've been through a war because I'm so stiff. It's like stone. When you start moving it loosens up. But to one degree or another, I'm stiff every morning.

I was lucky, though. There is no cure, but she said they caught the condition early enough to where they can keep it at this stage, and it won't get worse. I've been able to control it through medication and staying active. It might cause discomfort to exercise, but you need to exercise. You're not injuring yourself. You're actually making it better even if it hurts. In a way, it's the hurting part that's making it better. I've seen some pictures of people whose hands become gnarled or they end up in a wheelchair, so I'm grateful that neurologist caught it when he did.

People who don't really understand RA are always saying to me: *Why don't you relax?* or *You should ease up on your fitness regimen.* I believe if you stop moving, you're giving the RA an upper hand. As my rheumatologist explained, your antibodies keep attacking the joints and other places causing inflammation. When the tissue inside the joint becomes inflamed it eventually damages the joint's cartilage and bone. In turn the surrounding muscles, ligaments, and tendons become weakened. So if you just do a light treadmill workout, as if you're taking a walk around the block for thirty minutes, or a light jog, it doesn't do anything to relieve the muscle.

When I travel and they don't have a full gym, I'll just take a couple of thirty-minute walks. And I'll tell you after just two days my whole body stiffens up to where it's painful everywhere. So intense workouts are the best thing, at least for me. It loosens the ligaments and stretches and strengthens the muscles.

Just as importantly, it strengthens your bones. That's important because RA can lessen your bone density. So instead of a walk or light treadmill I'll really hammer the floor or jog or lift heavy weights. The irony is that everyone thinks I'm just working out so much because of my yearly DCC tryouts. But even if I never auditioned again, I would have to work out to keep my RA symptoms at bay.

My rheumatologist prescribed me Plaquenil, which is used to treat RA symptoms—and malaria, which will be handy if I decide to make a trip to North Africa. Plaquenil is considered a second-line medication. Thankfully, it works for me. The first-line medication is called Methotrexate, a cancer medication that is very caustic. It's very bad. It can lower your blood cell count and can damage your liver, lungs, or kidneys.

RA drugs suppress the immune system, which is your body's army. The Plaquenil is like the general saying: *Okay, calm down. Let's take the fighters off the frontlines.* When you take the frontline fighters off it helps reduce the inflammation, which is good for treating RA. However, it also makes you more susceptible to infections. I've noticed since going on the medication that I get more colds than I used to. But that's a tradeoff I'm happy to make.

I was curious how long I'd had RA before it was diagnosed. But there's no way for them to know for sure. It's possible I've had this all my life, and it just never became noticeable until I was in my forties.

I still keep up on RA advancements and research, but I haven't learned anything earth-shattering that the specialists haven't already told me. There's no miracle cure on the horizon, so the best option is to live a healthy lifestyle and stay active. And no, going gluten-free doesn't help. Gluten is a protein found in wheat, rye, and barley, and in many packaged and restaurant foods. If you have celiac disease and eat gluten, your small intestine gets inflamed, so you can't absorb some nutrients. RA is separate from that, and it has different causes. Apples and oranges.

I know some people find it beneficial to join support groups. Maybe because I'm a doctor and am trained to approach medical conditions more clinically than emotionally, or maybe because it's my nature to keep plowing forward, I've never sought out any support groups. Which is not to say I don't think they are helpful; it just wouldn't necessarily make a difference for me.

More than anything, I believe regular weight-bearing and aerobic exercise has helped me control my RA symptoms. The fact that the DCC tryouts give me additional incentive to be disciplined with exercising is just icing on the workout cake, especially as the day of the tryout draws nearer.

Thirty-Day Countdown

From audio journal, April 10, 2016

I'm going to start dictating some of my thoughts as I get closer and closer to auditions because so many different things go through my mind now. I use countdowns to help me mentally prepare for the physical and emotional rigors of trying out for the DCC. I used to do a twelve-week countdown to auditions, but thirty days is more focused.

What my thirty-day countdown consists of is blocking all unnecessary things from my schedule, looking ahead, and seeing what I can weed out. I'll also start a daily log of my food intake and how many calories I consume. I keep to a 1500-calorie a day during these last few weeks, and that is really hard to maintain because it can literally make me dizzy.

Most of the girls at the prep class on Friday night obviously have a dance background, probably since they were toddlers. If I couldn't do a chin-up as a kid, I can only imagine how I would have fared in dance class. But I digress ...

You can tell the dancers from the non-dancers; I definitely fall into the latter category. It was frustrating this last Friday because I had rolled my ankle and couldn't dance. Instead I did a lot of stretching. I was also allowed to sit at the front of the class and watch everybody.

A month out from the tryouts I find my mind starts reflecting on different things. For example, sitting there watching rehearsal I thought: *Wait a minute ... there are no other Chinese girls here. Just me.* Maybe we're not culturally predisposed to have rhythm. Or maybe our mothers were too busy keeping us home to make sure we achieved academically. That's the Chinese immigrant mindset. *Let's make sure this kid succeeds; let's make sure she gets to school and gets really high grades ... and she needs to be a doctor. We have to get ahead in this new country.*

Again, I digress ...

Watching the girls dance—girls I've seen week after week—I was struck by how groomed and ready to go they seem. They are ready to audition—tonight. They're primed for it. And that inspires me and motivates me. I love this whole process, the regimen, and the structure. And in my head I hear: *You have to do this; you* HAVE *to do this.* I love the competition.

Starting this week, I have two sessions with a professional trainer plus the workouts I do on my own. My solo training schedule was designed by a trainer at Southern Methodist University. And over the next thirty days I'll meet with my private choreographer. We actually started working together last September. He works at Power House Dance Studio. He's one of the instructors there, and I had watched him over the previous couple of years. He's been on *American Idol* and has worked in New York.

In September 2015 I went up to him and said, "Lonnie, you know I'm getting ready for the Cowboy Cheerleader tryouts, right?" Of course he'd have to be living under a rock not to know. "I'd like to hire you as my choreographer."

He agreed. So I hired him, he put together the routine, and we set up a schedule for him to teach it to me. So, we've been working on that since September or October. It is definitely the routine I'll use on May 14. The time from October until now has been spent learning it and perfecting it. Unfortunately, because of rolling my ankle I had to cancel my private lesson Thursday.

I also have a private high kick instructor that I meet with every week and who I'll continue to meet every week now leading into auditions. Yes, trainers are that specialized. And kicks are an integral part of the auditions. There is a surprising amount of mechanics involved with doing kicks properly ... especially when you're only pushing five feet tall. Some of those girls have legs that seem longer than I am tall. So I've just learned to think tall and channel my inner Rockette.

I've got the outfit all ready. In addition to the outfit you wear there, you also need to have back-up items: two back-up tops, two back-up shorts, three pairs of pantyhose, and two pairs of tennis shoes. We don't dance in the jazz shoes you see in dance classes. We use Nike Free Fits for the auditions because they slide. Those are the same shoes professionals like the Laker Girls and dance teams wear.

I don't want to have to think about having my outfit ready, so I spent yesterday packing everything, so that is ready to go. Yes, I know it's still four weeks away, but hey, like I always say, you never know if there's going to be a fire. So just in case, I'll have my bag ready to go.

Watch a fifty-year-old doctor train with teens for her shot at being a Dallas Cowboys cheerleader. [23, 24]

If Chiufang Hwang's name sounds slightly familiar, you might have seen her on TV being interviewed about trying out—yet again—to be a Dallas Cowboys cheerleader. The Dallas physician's first attempt was in 1999, when she was thirty-three. Just because she's now fifty is no reason to skip No. 10, which happens on May 14, 2016.

How/why into fitness?

Growing up in a Taiwanese family, my mother fed me a huge bowl of white rice every day for lunch and dinner. Even in my college years, she would not let me eat dinner on campus. She would bring a Corningware bowl of Chinese white rice drizzled with pork grease and a few beef tips for my dinner every night, and I'd sit in the passenger seat of her car and eat it. I got into nutrition to try to undo many unhealthy eating habits from my culture and add fitness, which was not part of my family's concept.

Typical week of workouts:

I do weights three times a week at the gym, swim ten freestyle laps each day with leg floats. Saturdays at 11 a.m., noon, and 1 p.m., I attend Saturday group classes at Dallas Power House of Dance with high-school girls. Twice a week, I also have private classes there.

If I had just twenty minutes to work out ...

I would do one hundred crunches and practice getting into my splits to prepare for tryouts.

What gets in the way of my exercise?

My disapproving Taiwanese parents, who discourage me, as well as having to let go of those Chinese cultural habits and ways of thinking.

Items you'll always find in my refrigerator:

A few pieces of chocolate, a carton of milk, coconut chews

Fitness goals:

To get in the best physical shape and memorize the dance routines to be a candidate for the Dallas Cowboys Cheerleaders.

Proudest fitness moment:

Last year, being a forty-nine-year-old auditioning alongside a couple of hundred very young girls for Dallas Cowboys cheerleaders, and yet no one questioned my age or abilities.

Favorite healthy food:

Milk

Favorite indulgence:

Chocolate

What I'd tell someone who wants to follow my routine:

Always print it out on a sheet of paper and carry it with you to the gym so you don't leave anything out.

What my workout says about me:

You can make the decision to undo unhealthy family habits and cultural ways that you have been accustomed to.

Chapter 6

Pumping Iron and High Kicks

As I mentioned earlier, I wasn't the most athletic child. Short and petite, most people considered me frail. It wasn't that I was sickly; it was that I never exercised, so I was about as toned as a garden slug. Running introduced me to the physical and emotional benefits of exercise, and as an adult I've made working out a part of my regular routine.

But there's exercise and then there's working out to prepare for a Dallas Cowboys Cheerleader audition. It's not just your ability to dance; you have to look the part. And it's not like you're standing up there alone in the room. Most of those who audition range in age between eighteen to twenty-five and are in peak physical condition. They're like my children's age, which is sobering. But I'm honestly not intimidated by that. Part of me loves it and uses it for motivation, so each year I put more time and preparation into it. I am twenty-five years older than everybody else, so I *have* to keep working out every day.

When I started back in 1999, I mostly just did the prep classes, which run for eight weeks. The organizers know most people work or go to school, so they schedule the classes at night. They used to be on Thursdays with two sessions: one from 7:00 to 8:30 and another 8:30 to 10:00. A fair number of girls would stay for both classes. But around 2007 they changed the classes to Friday nights and now only have one session, 7:00 to 9:00.

Each class costs forty-five dollars. I always pay in advance because if you just show up the class will likely be full. So as soon as they post the prep class dates in January, I pay for the nights I'll be there. Sometimes I know I'll be out of town on a given Friday, but for the most part I go to every class I can.

We spend the first fifteen or twenty minutes warming up and stretching. Sometimes they throw in a little ab work. Then about 7:30 the instructor starts teaching the class that week's routine and the group follows. In the past it used to be the same in-house instructor for all eight classes. But now they have outside dance instructors and choreographers each week. The routines they teach basically reflect the skills the DCC judges want to see: agility, rhythm, athleticism, enthusiasm, high-energy—in other words, it's exhausting. Each week is like a mini DCC boot camp.

The variety of instructors is good because you never get used to any one person's style. Sometimes it's very hip-hop, sometimes jazz-based—I felt like an extra from Bob Fosse's *Chicago* with all the jazz hands and kicks this one instructor had us doing.

It's been interesting to see how popular dance styles have changed over the years. Jazz moves were really common when I first started. Now it's like bump and grind and pop-n-lock. I don't think I'm getting any more proficient. Maybe if we started doing jazz again like when I first started out, I'd have it down by now. While it's admittedly a bit humbling to see how quickly these girls pick up every routine, I still love participating and challenging myself. If nothing else, I'd be a hit at all the dance clubs—not that I've actually ever been to one. (While

I have an insatiable curiosity about American pop culture I'm still clueless about much of it.)

For as hard as it is to learn a new routine every week, at least it's exciting. There's so much energy in the room. Regular exercise, on the other hand, can be very routine, very monotonous. I completely understand why a lot of people can't stick to it after maybe six months or a year. Or even a month. It's very boring if you do the same thing. The hardest thing about staying in shape isn't the physical part for most people; it's the mental aspect. It requires a lot of discipline. And if there's one thing anyone raised by a Taiwanese mother has, it's discipline. The discipline of working out is what I think I am most drawn to.

Plus, I've essentially been in training for so many years that if I stopped, I'm afraid I'd go through literal withdrawal. It's no joke when they talk about exercising becoming like a drug. Your endorphins are flying, and all kinds of good stuff is going on in your body. But more than anything, I'd miss the routine of my weekly workouts.

Another thing I find interesting about the prep classes is that while the faces change, it's still basically the same people: drill team captains, beauty queens, aspiring professional dancers, high school and college cheerleaders, actresses and models looking for the exposure being a DCC brings. What connects them all is that they are uniformly good dancers.

And every year there's almost a complete turnover. As of 2016, I will have been going fifteen years now and besides me, the maximum anyone's ever kept coming back is about three years; after that I don't see them anymore. Typically, if they don't make it the first time they'll come back to the next year's prep classes and try a second time. But if they don't make it then, most move on to pursue their careers in other ways.

There was one gal I saw in the prep classes who taught aerobics. She was a very, very good dancer and singer, and she tried out three years ago. She was small like me, slender, and had the hip moves down, the head swing going, and had that all-American blonde look—she had it all. In 2014, she made it to the finals but didn't make the team.

She didn't come back to class in 2015, but I happened to run into her in passing, and I was shocked. She just looked washed out, as if all the life had been drained from her. And it was like she'd completely let herself go and just didn't care anymore, as if getting so close only to get cut at the last minute had ruined her life or sent her into a mild depression. Or at the very least, prompted her to say the hell with working out for a while.

I guess it's like when you hear about actors getting all buff for some movie role with the six-pack abs and minus-two percent body fat. Then you see them doing publicity for the movie when it finally comes out, and they look nothing like the character anymore. They are motivated to train for that specific role then when it's done they just go back to being people. With most of the girls I meet in class, they're not there for the experience. They are not of the *it's just an honor to be nominated* mindset. Their only purpose for being there is to get chosen so they can put Dallas Cowboys cheerleader on their résumé and be on the *Making the Team* TV series. So when they don't make it, many figure there's no reason to keep killing—and starving—themselves training. They go back to teaching Zumba and are content.

I can't say I blame them. If I didn't have RA, who knows if I'd be as disciplined as I am now doing these workouts ... okay, who am I kidding? Of course I would be, but I freely admit I'm a bit OCD. (Another thing to thank my mother for.) Plus, I'm all about the experience; it puts me side-by-side with a variety of people and a different subculture of American girls that I never got to be with. The result is really secondary.

My physical training consists of choreography, exercise, and kick instruction with Lauren, who is a high-kick and drill instructor at Powerhouse. She was a Kilgore College Rangerette. Kilgore is a two-year college in East Texas known for having the world's first women's precision drill team, and I was impressed when I read about their history.

In 1939, Kilgore dean, Dr. B.E. Masters, decided the college needed an organization that would attract young women. His goal of equalizing the male/female student ratio had a secondary benefit: the folks would stay in the stands during halftime instead of sipping improper beverages under them.

According to the Texas State Historical Association:[25]

Dr. Masters brought Miss Gussie Nell Davis, a physical education teacher, to Kilgore College to create something special. Davis, who had established the Flaming Flashes, a high school girls' drum and bugle corps in Greenville in 1928, enlisted the help of local oil millionaire Liggett Crim to pay for the Rangerettes' initial costs.

The first group of its kind in the world, the Rangerettes brought show business to the football gridiron. The group became popular locally after its debut in September 1940. Its fame promptly spread outside Kilgore, and within a year the Rangerettes had traveled to New Orleans to represent the region's oil business at the Lions International convention. The Rangerettes began appearing throughout East Texas in bond shows in support of the war effort. They have continued to perform for the college and have also participated in many other athletic and special events, such as the Cotton Bowl ... the Macy's Thanksgiving Day Parade, and the American Bar Association Convention. Since the 1970s they have taken six world tours to South America, the Far East, Romania, France, Canada, and Japan.

Members of the troupe are selected each August at a two-week tryout camp, during which as many as 150 applicants vie for some thirty openings. Normally sixty-five students make up the team, but only forty-eight members actually perform at one time. Known for well-choreographed routines, including its trademark high kick, the troupe thrived under the direction of Gussie Davis for almost four decades, until her retirement in 1979. She was responsible for turning the Rangerettes into a company that executed perfect routines by holding to the concept that the Rangerettes *don't make mistakes.*

The Rangerettes have historically been identified with one costume, made up of a blouse, arm gauntlets, a belt, and a short circular skirt, in red, white, and blue. A white hat and boots complete the Rangerette look. The costume has remained unchanged, except for a slight shortening of the skirt length.

To underscore the significance of the Kilgore Rangerettes, Kilgore College opened a Rangerette Showcase on its campus in 1979. The exhibit, housed in the college's physical education building, features costumes, props, and other memorabilia. A sixty-seat theater in the building provides films and slide shows on Rangerette performances.

Sounds like a down-home version of the Cowboys cheerleaders, doesn't it? Probably not so coincidentally, the Rangerettes actually performed at a Cowboys game in 2013. In Texas it's more like two degrees of separation. Anyway, as soon as I read about those high kicks, I hired Lauren pretty much year-round, especially for when we're just a few months away from the tryout, and we do kicks, kicks, and more kicks. Around-the-world kicks, high kicks, exercise kicks. We go through all those because she knows what the judges are looking for. We work together once a week, and then I practice on my own until our next session.

I start by stretching, paying particular attention on my hamstrings and hip flexors. It's important to take your time so you don't pull anything. Trust me; I've made that mistake. It's always been minor, but a serious injury will set you back, so don't rush. Whether you're learning kicks or splits, working on it every week will show results.

I'm also supposed to meet with my choreographer once a week as well, but it hasn't always turned out that way. In the past, I've hired people who can choreograph a routine, but it's too stiff and doesn't give me what I want. So, it's a toss-up between hiring a choreographer who can give you a so-so routine and meet you once a week like clockwork but who's not that good, or someone that's innovative and creative but has a busier schedule because they are in demand so you might not always be able to meet at a set time every week.

Also, great talent often means higher ambition. I've had choreographers say: *Sorry. I have to go to New York for four weeks, 'cause I'm rehearsing with the Alvin Ailey Dance Theater.* I'm not the most patient person, but I've learned to deal with it because the end result is worth the annoyance.

The other part of my regimen is strength training and toning. In interviews, I'm often asked what my favorite exercise is. Honestly, it's all the same to me. There are no pros or cons. I'm kind of neutral. I do weights, but I don't love it or hate it. I just know I need to do it to get tone and definition. I'll tell you what I do like: the endorphin head and body rush I get when I hit that certain level of exertion. It's funny that I never got a runner's high during cross-country; probably because it came so easy to me I never felt I was overly exerting myself. Had I known, I might have run a lot harder.

My fitness regimens have evolved over the years as my fitness has improved. Here are my workouts for February and March of 2016. For as challenging as this schedule is, it's not the hardest part of preparing for tryouts. The biggest challenge is not leaving the workout and heading straight to the nearest In-N-Out Burger.

FEBRUARY					
Date	Exercises	Sets	Reps	Weight	Stretches
1	Decline Sit-up	3	8	8	Single Lunge
	Bench Press	3	3	20	Side Bend
	Incline Leg Raise	3	10	2aw (ankle wgts)	Back Arch
	Deadlift	3	10	50bb (barbell)	Single Hamstring
	Swiss Plank	3	3	20″	Pigeon
3	Swiss Ball Pike	3	12	0	Twist
	Chin-ups	3	11	−25	Eagle
	Arch March	3	8	2aw	Side Lunge
	Squat	3	3	30bb	Down Dog
	Side Plank	3	50″	0	Arms Overhead
5	Russian Twist	3	12	5′	Standing Eagle Touch Floor
	Sitting Military Press	3	12	17	Lying Knee to Chest
	Mountain Climber(Floor)	3	3	0	Double Hamstring Sitting
	Lunge	3	3	12	Child's Pose
	Med Ball Cycle	3	12	5	Cat-Cow
8	Lateral Raise	3	3	10	Touch Floor
	Calves Sitting	3			Butterfly
	Decline Sit-up	3	10	8	Lying Twist
	Bench Press	3	5	20	Both Knees to Chest
	Incline Leg Raise	3	12	2aw	Gastroc
10	Deadlift	3	12	50bb	Soleus
	Plank Swiss	3	25″	0	Standing Quad
	Swiss Ball Pike	3	15	0	Standing Single Hamstring
	Chin-ups	3	12	−25	Lying Hamstring with Rope
	Arch March	3	10	2aw	Arms Behind Back
12	Squat	3	5	30bb	Single Lunge
	Slide Plank	3	55″	0	Side Bend
	Russian Twist	3	15	5′	Back Arch
	Sitting Military Press	3	15	17	Single Hamstring
	Mountain Climber	3	5	0	Pigeon

Date	Exercises	Sets	Reps	Weight	Stretches
15	Lunge	3	5	12	Twist
	Lateral Raise	3	5	10	Eagle
	Gastroc Heel Raise	3	15	0	Side Lunge
	Decline Sit-up	3	12	8	Down Dog
	Bench Press	3	8	20	Arms Overhead
17	Incline Leg Raise	3	15	2aw	Standing Eagle Touch Floor
	Deadlift	3	15	50bb	Lying Knee to Chest
	Plank Swiss	3	30″	0	Double Hamstring Sitting
	Swiss Ball Pike	3	20	0	Child's Pose
	Chin-ups	3	13	−25	Cat-Cow
19	Workout at Dedman Rec with Emily				
22	Arch March	3	12	2aw	Soleus
	Squat	3	8	30bb	Standing Quad
	Side Plank	3	1′	0	Standing Single Hamstring
	Russian Twist	3	3	8lbs	Lying Hamstring w/ Rope
	Sitting Military Press	3	3	20	Arms Behind Back
24	Mountain Climber	3	8	0	Single Lunge
	Lunge	3	8	12	Side Bend
	Lateral Raise	3	8	10	Back Arch
	Gastroc Heel Raise	3	15	0	Single Hamstring
	Decline Sit-up	3	15	8	Pigeon
26	Bench Press	3	10	20	Twist
	Incline Leg Raise	3	3	3aw	Eagle
	Deadlift	3	3	Bar + 10 lbs. = 55	Side Lunge
	Plank Swiss	3		3 x 45″	Down Dog
	Swiss Ball Pike	3	3	5″ holds	Arms Overhead
29	Chin-ups	3	14	25	Standing Eagle Touch Flr
	Arch March	3	15	2aw	Lying Knee to Chest
	Squat	3	10	30bb	Double Hamstring Sitting
	Side Plank	3	15″	leg lift	Child's Pose
	Russian Twist	3	5	8lbs	Cat-Cow

MARCH					
Date	**Exercises**	**Sets**	**Reps**	**Weight**	**Stretches**
2	Mountain Climber	3	10		Single Lunge
	Standing Calves	3	3	20	Side Bend
	Wood Chop	3	3	comfortable	Back Arch
	Shrugs	3	12	20	Single Hamstring
	Ab Roller	3	8		Pigeon
4	Superman	3	12		Twist
	Cable Sit Row	3	10	55	Eagle
	Jack knife	3	10		Side Lunge
	Cable Single Leg	3	8	20	Down Dog
	Incline Leg Up	3	15		Arms Overhead
7	Side Plank on Bench	3	5″	90° or less	Standing Eagle Touch Floor
	Lying Tri Pulls	3	10	25	Lying Knee to Chest
	Russian Twist	3	5	8	Double Hamstring Sitting
	Calves Sitting	3	15	110 Total*	Child's Pose
	Med Ball Cycle	3	15	5	Cat-Cow
9	Plank on Swiss	3	50″		Touch Floor
	Dips	3	15	(55)	Butterfly
	Swiss Ball Pike	3	5	5″ hold	Lying Twist
	Squat	3	10	30bb	Both Knees to Chest
	Dec Sit-up	3	3	8	Gastroc
11	Dedman Rec with Emily				
14	Mountain Climber	3	12		Single Lunge
	Standing Calves	3	5	20	Side Bend
	Wood Chop	3	5	comfortable*	Back Arch
	Shrugs	3	15	20	Single Hamstring
	Ab Roller	3	10		Pigeon
16	Superman	3	15		Twist
	Cable Sit Row	3	12	55	Eagle
	Jack knife	3	12		Side Lunge
	Cable Single Leg	3	10	20	Down Dog
	Incline Leg Up	3	3	2aw*	Arms Overhead

Date	Exercises	Sets	Reps	Weight	Stretches
18	Side Plank on Bench	3	10″	90° or less	Standing Eagle Touch Floor
	Lying Tri Pulls	3	12	25	Lying Knee to Chest
	Russian Twist	3	8	8	Double Hamstring Sitting
	Calves Sitting	3	3	110 Total*	Child's Pose
	Med Ball Cycle	3	3	8	Cat-Cow
21	Plank on Swiss	3	55′		Standing Eagle Touch Floor
	Dips	3	4	3w/(−55)+2w/(0)*	Lying Knee to Chest
	Swiss Ball Pike	3	8	5″ hold	Double Hamstring Sitting
	Squat	3	12	30bb	Child's Pose
	Dec Sit-up	3	5	8	Cat-Cow
22	Mountain Climber	3	15		Soleus
	Standing Calves	3	8	20	Standing Quad
	Wood Chop	3	8	comfortable*	Standing Single Hamstring
	Shrugs	3	3	25	Lying hamstring with Rope
	Ab Roller	3	12		Arms Behind Back
23	Superman	3	20		Single Lunge
	Cable Sit Row	3	15	55	Side Bend
	Jack knife	3	15		Back Arch
	Cable Single Leg	3	12	20	Single Hamstring
	Incline Leg Up	3	5	2aw*	Pigeon
25	Side Plank on Bench	3	15″	90° or less	Twist
	Lying Tri Pulls	3	15	25	Eagle
	Russian Twist	3	10	8	Side Lunge
	Calves Sitting	3	5	110 Total*	Down Dog
	Med Ball Cycle	3	5	8	Arms Overhead
28	Plank on Swiss	3	1′		Standing Eagle Touch Floor
	Dips	3	5	3w/(−55)+2w/(0)*	Lying Knee to Chest
	Swiss Ball Pike	3	10	5″ hold	Double Hamstring Sitting
	Squat	3	15	30bb	Child's Pose
	Dec Sit-up	3	8	8	Cat-Cow

Date	Exercises	Sets	Reps	Weight	Stretches
30	Mountain Climber	3	1ea	Swiss Ball	Standing Eagle Touch Floor
	Standing Calves	3	10	20	Lying Knee to Chest
	Wood Chop	3	10	comfortable*	Double Hamstring Sitting
	Shrugs	3	5	25	Child's Pose
	Ab Roller	3	15		Cat-Cow

Dallas Cowboys Cheerleader Tryouts Tips

Over the years I've picked up a lot of dos and don'ts while at the tryouts. Here are some tips to keep you from getting the wrong kind of attention.

★ If you have a tattoo, cover it up with concealer if it's visible while wearing your outfit. Nobody there is against self-expression, but should you make the team, they want the uniform to be the attraction, not your ink.

★ Don't ask to see the judges' sheets to find out their comments or your score. They are not for public consumption. Judges need to be brutally honest in their assessment, and that would be hard to do knowing the participant would be reading it later.

★ While there are no specific dance moves you have to do at the preliminary audition, you'll be well served to include a little hip-hop along with jazz elements. Kelli calls the Cheerleaders' performance style precision, jazz-based dancing. With pom-poms.

★ Smile. Never stop. Smile until your jaw feels like it's turned to concrete. Nobody wants a sourpuss cheerleader.

★ If your mind goes blank during your routine, don't stop. Just keep doing … something. The worst thing you could so is skulk off the dance floor while the music is still going. Take a second to compose yourself if need be, then just fake it. Being able to think on your suddenly leaden feet shows your character and poise. Public meltdowns are not the DCC way.

★ Leave the family at home. Even though the auditions

will eventually be seen by millions of strangers on the TV series, auditions are closed to the public.

★ Make a good first impression. Here's what a former participant advises: "During each of round of auditions, when you walk onto the dance floor ... each person introduces themselves to the judges. We call your introduction a *slate*. It should be short and concise, but you also want to provide a glimpse of who you are. So you say your name, your age, where you're from, and something short that is interesting. If you're in school, or if you have an interesting career, or if you have a parent in the military, you want to mention something that may differentiate you from everyone else. You don't want to ramble, but you want to give the judges something to remember."[26]

Chapter 7

Total Blockout

From audio journal, April 29, 2016 ...

We're ten days out from the audition and I'm in what I call my Total Blockout, where I consume 1200 calories or less. A day. I feel like I've become a lot more alert, like I'm on a constant adrenaline rush. It's like every second is fight or flight. I have a new appreciation for what the cavemen must have gone through on slow hunting and gathering days. And oddly, I also feel like I have a lot more energy. Either that or it's delirium from hunger.

I was thinking today how my appearance fools you. I come across as a very professional, classy lady, a medical doctor. A *psychiatrist*, no less. But the moment someone tries to shortchange me or get one up on me—or even if I just think they are—then my street comes out. Only someone who's grown up on the streets can know what that's like. The bottom falls right out of my stately demeanor and *wham*, out comes my tough-talking reaction; *boom*, just like that I'm back on the streets of Columbia with my bus-riding buddy, Janine.

When I react in unexpected ways, even those who've known me for years can't figure out why I do that. People are taken aback. It's my street side. I've discovered that hunger brings it out even more.

103

May 3

I'm so calorie deprived that I've gotten very antsy. Very hyper. It's almost like a state of crisis. When you're in a crisis, you don't know what's going to hit next. Right now I'm hungry. I'm very hungry because I have to cut down more weight. When you're on in front of the camera, it adds weight to your appearance. This morning I weighed in at 97.6 pounds, which is good. It fluctuates during the day, but as long as I stay at one hundred pounds or less I'm good.

The problem with being so tiny is that every ounce shows up. I'm not big-boned either. I'm a tiny person. So three pounds will show up immediately. And in all the wrong places. They want to see your muscle definition when they take your photo or when you're on stage—especially with someone my age. They want to see the cut. Plus, I want to blend in with everyone. And everyone there is toned with lots of definition.

It's kind of hard to sleep because I don't have any calories in my system, which also makes you very edgy. And did I mention irritable?

During those last couple of weeks before the audition, I admit I get a little snappy. I think part of it is sleep deprivation. I'll wake up with a start about two or three in the morning, worried that I've slept through my alarm. Once I get my bearings, I'll just lie there and try to relax so I can fall back to sleep. But I'm starving and have to keep myself from raiding the refrigerator. *You just have to not get up. If you go pee, go pee, but if you don't, just lie there until you fall back.* That happens almost every night.

Then during the day, the challenge is not to go street on people, so I have to be vigilant. I almost fired someone because I could sense she was going to ask me for a raise. So I asked if there was something she wanted to talk to me about.

She started off with some questions about paperwork then summoned the courage to say she felt she deserved a raise. I asked on what basis she'd come to that conclusion. She said she had checked around and other clinics paid more for her position. My face went stone cold, that serious face with the beady, dragon lady eyes. She was shocked because she'd never seen my street side before.

I told her: *I don't know where you got your information, but let me give you the facts. You have a gravy train from us. You do not have to hustle for these patients. You work two days a week at your choosing. You come and go as you please, and you are highly overpaid. If you or anyone working in this clinic feel like you can get a higher salary somewhere else—or you don't like being here, or you're not comfortable here, or you simply don't want to be here—you can leave right at this minute. Right this second. You don't have to give me a two weeks' notice.*

Did I mention I get really snappy when I'm hungry?

The poor woman got so quiet. She looked like she'd seen a ghost because I'm sure I seemed otherworldly at that moment. But that response was directly related to my total blockout. Now, I would have turned her down even if I was stuffing my face with a cheeseburger. But because I was on a low calorie regimen, I was a lot more serious, and the street, stone face came out.

Apparently, I scared the entire staff because they were so quiet. No doubt worried they were going to set the crazy lady off. I finally came out and said: *Hey, you guys don't have to worry. You guys are okay. Just wanted to let you know.*

The thing is, they all know about me trying out for the DCC because there's been quite a bit of press on me that last couple of years as I inch towards fifty. A month before the audition, an article came out on Reuters that a surprising number of people apparently saw.

Chiufang H. Hwang, M.D., wife, mother of two and aspiring author, is training and preparing for the upcoming Dallas Cowboys Cheerleader tryouts on May 14, 2016. Dr. Hwang has tried out to become one of America's Sweethearts ten times over the years, and at fifty years old, she is more determined than ever.

"The Dallas Cowboys Cheerleaders are an outstanding

organization," said Dr. Hwang. "They are well-known and respected all over the world, even in my home country of Taiwan. It has always been a dream of mine to make the team, and everyone has always been very supportive and motivating. I truly enjoy the competition and look forward to the entire tryout experience each year."

Dr. Hwang began her training regimen three months leading up to the tryouts. She has hired a choreographer to teach her a dance routine, a high-kick instructor to help her with her fan kicks, attends weekly Dallas Cowboys Cheerleader prep classes at Valley Ranch, and follows a strict exercise routine and nutrition plan.

Dr. Hwang's journey hasn't always been easy. In 2012, she was diagnosed with rheumatoid arthritis (RA), affecting the joints in both of her hands and feet. Although there is no known cure for RA, she is currently taking medication to manage her joint pain, and it hasn't stopped her from pursuing her dream.

"The competition is very demanding, but I enjoy the challenge of performing and meeting the criteria," Dr. Hwang added. "I give 110 percent in everything I do. People are always asking if I have made the team. No, but I keep on trying!"

Over the years, Dr. Hwang has become a news topic and has been recognized for her journey to become a Dallas Cowboys Cheerleader on FOX Sports and the Meredith Viera Show.

So my staff was aware I was in the home stretch. A lot of people were. Many acquaintances came up to me saying: "Hey, I hope you get it this year. I'm rooting for you."

And I'd look at them wondering: *Do they not know that I really can't dance too well?*

Then they'd add, "Oh, I just know this is your lucky year!"

And I'm thinking, *No, they have no clue.*

But I understand it. They want to see the underdog succeed. If

I can achieve the seeming impossible, then maybe they can achieve something they've always dreamed of doing. Just me making the effort is inspiring to them. Getting out of my comfort zone to learn a routine and dance in front of a roomful of people gives me a sense of accomplishment that only comes from just going for it. I think everyone has something they've always wanted to do. I hope I can encourage them to go do it. What's the worst that can happen? Failing? By just showing up you win.

Of course in my case, I show up starving. Okay, that may be a bit dramatic because it's not like I eat a whole lot more normally. I think it's as much a matter of what I'm eating as it is watching calories at a time I'm also working out a lot.

During my total blockout, instead of a regular breakfast, all I drank was coffee, with a little cream or milk. Then between breakfast and lunch, around 10:00 or 11:00 a.m., I'd drink a sixteen-ounce glass of water—or tea, just to give me some flavor. Then I'd eat a big lunch at the cafeteria in our building. A typical lunch would be two slices of brisket, vegetables, and maybe a carb, like couscous. I'd also have some bread with it.

I savored those lunches because it felt so good to eat. And afterward I'd feel very satiated. That was it until a small dinner. I ate very little at night. Maybe a little piece of fish with avocado and some vegetables. I'm not real picky. Nor am I the anal type who measures and weighs everything. I just eat the healthiest option of whatever is available. I often stop at a takeout café on my way home and get their California burger, which has all white turkey meat, an avocado slice, and tomatoes. I would eat that until I was kind of full—usually just half of it. And that's a typical example of my 1,200 calories or less a day.

I'm sometimes amazed that I eat as healthfully as I do considering my background. As I mentioned, my mother wasn't worried about giving us a well-balanced diet. We were mostly stuck with white rice. My mother had her Chinese rice cooker going all day long. She made sure that cooker was always full, so we could just go scoop out our own rice when we were hungry. As a result, we often had rice at every meal. I've always wondered if that's one reason I'm barely five feet tall.

In the morning we'd have white rice porridge with pickled cucumbers. In the evening, white rice with green beans and pork sausage, the kind they hang in the window at Chinese markets that you can see the little pieces of fat in them. It's so good but so heavy. A little goes a long way. And I'm sure that little bit went straight to set up shop in my arteries. Adding to my plaque buildup were the grease drippings from cooking the sausage that my mother mixed in with the rice. I don't think I ever heard of kale until I was in college.

Sometimes we would have a soft pastry called *youtiao* that's also known as a Chinese cruller, a Chinese oil stick, a Chinese doughnut … you get the idea. It's a long stick of fried dough. I prefer to think of it as a Chinese churro. On weekends for breakfast, we would dip it in hot soy milk—a much better option than rice porridge, flavor-wise.

You'd think that I would have learned to cook out of self-defense if for no other reason. But Mom would never let me in the kitchen. She did not think the kitchen was going to get me anywhere in life. *You're gonna go study. Out of the kitchen. Go study. You'll be a doctor, you'll be able to afford to buy food, don't worry.* I actually thank her for that. And to this day I do pretty much just buy our dinner on the way home.

When my kids were young I used Schwan's Home Delivery service. A lot. You would look through their catalogue and choose between hundreds of entrees and complete meals. Then you would order what you wanted and a refrigerated truck would pull up and deliver your meals. It was basically gourmet frozen food. But it was certainly much better than what you'd get at the grocery store. And even if I did cook, which I don't, I didn't get home until 6:00 or 6:30 in the evening, so I had to delegate dinner.

While I don't follow a specific diet, I am mindful that what I eat can have an impact on my RA. For example, research suggests eating fruits, veggies, whole grains, healthy fats, beans, and fish—what now has become known as a Mediterranean diet—can help control RA symptoms because those foods include chemicals that keep inflammation in check. Veggies, beans, and whole grains are also healthy because they're high in fiber. And fish is a good source of omega-3 fatty acids. If you have RA, olive oil can also lower levels of the chemicals that cause inflammation.

The rule of thumb is to eat a good variety of fruits and vegetables that have deep or bright colors, which generally indicates higher antioxidant levels. So anyone with RA should try to include blueberries, blackberries, squash, sweet potatoes, carrots, tomatoes, peppers, oranges, broccoli, and melons in their diet. Yes, medication is very important, but it can't hurt to complement medical science with a healthy diet. I read about one study that found women with RA who ate this way for six months had less joint pain and morning stiffness, and better overall health, than those who didn't. I figure it can't hurt; it can only help.

Ginger is also known to ease inflammation. Ginger has been used in Chinese cuisine for centuries and diet could be one factor in why RA strikes Asians as a group much less frequently than white populations.

One thing I've found that helps distract me from my total blockout calorie curbing is to enjoy the interest people have in how many times I've tried out for the DCC. I love it every time I get a call from a local news outlet asking if they can do a story on me for the evening news or an article for their publication. I'm sure some people see it as pure self-promotion, and maybe that's part of it; I've never denied I enjoy the attention, or that it makes me feel like one of the popular kids I watched from the other side of my high school cafeteria.

But I also hope I can empower women and inspire them to pursue their own impossible dream. You're never too old to and the only thing holding you back is you. That is something I repeat with every interview I give. Maybe the novelty of a fifty-year-old Chinese-American psychiatrist trying out to be an NFL cheerleader is enough to make them read the article, and maybe learning about my journey will spark them to think: *Why not?*

Doctor Never Quits Trying to Become Cowboys Cheerleader [27]

It's tough becoming a Dallas Cowboys cheerleader. Some of the best dancers from across the country and world came to AT&T Stadium last week for a chance to make the team. Among the more than five hundred hopefuls was someone who doesn't exactly fit the typical profile of an NFL cheerleader.

Dr. Chiufang Hwang is a forty-nine-year-old Dallas physician originally from Taiwan with no professional dancing experience, but that hasn't stopped her from auditioning for more than a decade.

"The first time I tried out for the Dallas Cowboys Cheerleaders in 1999, I was thirty-four years old," she said. "I do not have a dance background, but I just like being here and I love competition."

Being at least eighteen years old is the only age requirement to audition. The oldest Cowboys Cheerleader to ever make the team was thirty-seven years old.

"I'm here to promote women and empower women," Cowboys Cheerleader director Kelli Finglass told the entire group on Day 1 of the auditions. "Who cares what age you are?"

Hwang has never made it past the first round of cuts and has lost track of how many times she's auditioned, but it's been a few years since her last attempt.

Despite her age she felt more prepared than ever this time around. "I got a choreographer to put together a routine for me," she said. "I listen to the Top 40 music a lot more."

Behind the Scenes at Cowboys Cheerleader Auditions

"I think the main thing is the image and weight. You have to keep the weight down. You have to look the part, so I've been doing a lot of weight training. I put a lot more time and preparation into it this year."

Even with all the hard work she's put in, Hwang still doesn't think she can beat out girls half her age who have been training their entire lives. However, she hopes the judges will see more than what she can do on the dance floor.

"They're looking for a very experienced dancer," she said. "They're all more highly qualified than I am, but it may open up other opportunities being in front of the judges. This is the best time to be exposed."

Hwang will never give up trying and said she would continue to audition into her sixties. But making the team isn't the ultimate goal. She's already achieved what she's set out to do by just being a part of the audition process.

"Next year I'll be fifty. I hope they keep letting me come back and don't put on an age limit."

Forty-Nine-Year-Old Auditions for Dallas Cowboys Cheerleaders [28]

A Collin County doctor is proving you're never too old to pursue your dreams.

Chiufang Hwang spent the last three months, lifting, lunging, and learning dance routines to prepare. She stood out among more than five hundred women auditioning at AT&T Stadium to become a Dallas Cowboys Cheerleader.

"I am twenty-five years older than everybody else is," says Hwang. "I have to keep working out every day. It's probably unrealistic to think that I'm going to make the team."

You would think Doctor Hwang would be content just being a successful psychiatrist. But her Chinese heritage made her long for something uniquely American.

"When I was growing up I never went to any football games,"

Hwang says. "Other people have goals. They want to climb Mount Everest; they want to run the San Francisco Marathon. I want to audition for the Dallas Cowboys Cheerleaders."

Despite high kicks and splits better than many women half her age, Hwang didn't make the final cut last weekend.

But she promises to be back next year at age fifty.

(DALLAS) April 18, 2016 — Chiufang H. Hwang, M.D., wife, mother of two and aspiring author, is training and preparing for the upcoming Dallas Cowboys Cheerleader tryouts on May 14, 2016. Dr. Hwang has tried out to become one of America's Sweethearts ten times over the years, and at fifty years old, she is more determined than ever.

"The Dallas Cowboys Cheerleaders are an outstanding organization," said Dr. Hwang. "They are well-known and respected all over the world, even in my home country of Taiwan. It has always been a dream of mine to make the team, and everyone has always been very supportive and motivating. I truly enjoy the competition and look forward to the entire tryout experience each year."

"The competition is very demanding, but I enjoy the challenge of performing and meeting the criteria," Dr. Hwang added. "I give 110 percent in everything I do. People are always asking if I have made the team. No, but I keep on trying!"

Chapter 8

A Full Dance Card

I realize that it probably seems like I spend most of my days and weeks focusing solely on the yearly tryout. While the tryouts are a very big part of my personal goals, it's a small part of my daily life. I'm not a bored housewife who spends the day at the gym while my husband is at work. I have to carefully schedule my time to integrate DCC-related activities.

My kids are grown now, but even when they were little I wasn't a carpooling, soccer mom. I drove my kids to school before the sun came up and was always the first waiting for the janitor or principal to open the door because I had to be at work or was on call. They didn't do after-school activities either, but they played golf and tennis on the weekends because that's when I could schedule the time in.

I still work full time. All the time. That work ethic instilled in me as a kid by my mother, where school became my job, remains a fundamental part of my character. For example, there's no such thing as vacation. Even without the DCC there was no such thing as vacation. I don't even know what the word means. When I was growing up, my brother and I would be like: *Oh no, Christmas vacation* because it meant more math studying than when we were in school.

So when someone casually asks what I have planned for the weekend, sometimes that question strikes me like: *What do you mean, have I got plans? I have to catch up on work because I have to get ready for Monday.* I'm glad there's a weekend because if there wasn't I wouldn't be able to catch up on work. I use my weekends to go through my briefcase, organize what needs to be done, identify what needs to be settled, determine who I need to assign certain tasks to, and select what charts need to be reviewed, so I'm prepared when I walk into the office Monday morning. That is what will help me stay successful or become more successful.

Over the years I have stayed involved with some of the reunions. Then when my son was applying to medical school, I realized I needed to find out what was going on in medical education, so I could help him. That's when I decided: *I need to join my alumni board,* which I did around 2014. I'm basically a new member.

My purpose in going to the alumni board wasn't so much because I was concerned about the school; I want to get both of my sons into medical school, and I want to be able to watch them and get them into very successful careers. My mom wanted me to be a doctor; well, I want to crank out two physicians.

Oh, God, we really do turn into our mothers, don't we?

That cheery thought aside, once I became a regular presence around alumni functions and joined the alumni board, I guess because I'm very presentable and an eloquent speaker, people came to me and said: *Hey, we need this done.* Once I hear that, I'm on it. I have it done. It's already emailed. From there it just expanded to: *Hey, can you do this too?*

Eventually I set up a Dallas chapter for the local alumni, so it's in my town now. All of us alumni in Dallas meet about twice a year. It was after our son got admitted to our medical school alma mater in 2015 that I set up a program for the parents of the first year students that is now really tight. Based on my work in those areas, they asked me to speak at the white coat ceremony, which is for the incoming class.

I had one person tell me: "That speech was so moving and so traumatic, it was so compelling, that you'd just think: *My, God, that gal's gone through all that, and she's still standing there? If that gal is standing up there giving the speech, I have no excuse for complaining or not getting to where I need to be 'cause she's gone through all that, and she's standing there alive, and she made it.*"

I think what appeals to people is that I'm honest, and I really do speak from the heart. I know a lot of people prefer to keep their private life private; they believe it's not suitable for public consumption. But I'm not embarrassed to talk about my RA, nor do I feel my sister's cancer is something too hurtful to keep hidden. I feel that just gives it too much power over you. Plus, these are among the experiences that taken together inform who I am, for better or worse. If the idea is to inspire young people starting out in the world, showing them that if I can overcome disease and loss, they can overcome whatever challenges they will face as well.

I have no doubts my parenting style was influenced by my own upbringing. Just like at work, I was what I called a military mom when my boys were young. *Get this done, and this done, and that done.* I was very tough on both of my boys in that way. I'm not an easy mom. But I know how much discipline it takes to succeed, especially in medicine.

Back after the clinic started and the boys were young, like seven and eight years old, Doc usually didn't get home until 9:00 p.m. or later. But one night, he came home early and walked in as I was giving orders like a drill sergeant on what the boys needed to get done. He opened the door and was standing there like: *Man, what's going on?* He had never seen me in military mom mode. He just took it for granted that our boys were always respectful and polite and did their homework on time, as if they were just born that way.

In my defense, while I might have stressed education as much as my parents, I never made our boys spend the summer learning advanced mathematics textbooks. They got to participate in all the school activities I didn't get to. They did not grow up feeling they were on the outside looking in or stuck between two cultures. They are proud of their heritage but they are American kids with a military mom who participates in cheerleading tryouts—which, by the way, they think is pretty cool.

As you've probably picked up, I tend to have a sarcastic sense of humor. I often talk about how conservative Doc is—and he is—but he may not be quite the boogeyman I paint him to be when it comes to my participation in the cheerleading tryouts. But he's quiet and serious and can seem stern.

This week I went to the Cooper Aerobics Center, which is one of the places I work out. And I haven't been there in a while because I've been training at that dance studio. So when I walked into the women's locker room, I saw a woman I've known for probably twenty years. She knows Doc too. She came running to me in the locker room.

"Hey, I saw you in the *Dallas Morning News*. It's so great, and I sent the article to my son. And I said: *Remember this lady? You know, when you guys were little, she used to work out here? Look what she's doing.*"

And then she came up real close. "How are you keeping all this away from Doc? They showed it everywhere. It's in the news and everywhere. How did you get away from him?"

I said, "Well, every time the *Dallas Morning News* article came up, when one of his friends said: *Hey, I saw your wife in the paper,* I immediately said: *Oh, they were curious about our culture.* I just frame it in that context."

She seemed very relieved. "Oh, that's so good. You know what? When you get home every day, when you're around him just wrap yourself in a big apron."

Which, considering my cooking skills, was pretty funny.

Later on she said, "But what about at work? Surely, some colleagues must pal around and say: *Hey, what do you think about your wife trying to be a cheerleader?* How does he handle it?"

I actually didn't know how to answer that so she said, "You know what? He may not pal around with people in the clinic when he's busy working anyway."

I did send my kids the clip from the NBC news story and the *Dallas Morning News.* The one in San Antonio texted me back: *Oh mom, I hope you get it this year.* I was tempted to call him and say: *You know I've been doing it for sixteen years, right?* But I didn't. My other son responded: *Hey, that's good coverage.*

Boy after my own heart.

The truth is, Doc isn't quite as unaware of the DCC as it may seem. Around 2003 or so I took him to one of the cheerleaders' friends and family shows that features the squad from the football season that recently ended. It took place around April. It's not intended for the general public, so you had to know someone involved to get tickets. I knew someone and bought two tickets.

I told my husband we had to go to this show. It was held in an auditorium and when we arrived, there was a line filled with parents and other family members. Just regular folks like you'd see at the mall on Saturday. Once we finally got inside, I headed straight to get front-center seats with Doc in tow.

Then I heard someone say, "Dr. Hwang?"

Both me and my husband turned our heads at the same time. Of course I assumed they were talking to me. But then this young, attractive woman in the audience waves at Doc and again says, "Hi, Dr. Huang!"

He just froze, looking freaked out, and then said, "Jocelyn?"

He went over to talk to her—did I mention she was very attractive?—while I secured seats. I didn't know who she was. Turns out Jocelyn was one of his pharmaceutical reps.

When he came and sat down, Doc kind of sunk in his seat

because somebody in the audience knew him, but he watched the show intently. During the intermission he said, "Jocelyn asked me if my wife was a Cowboy cheerleader. And I said: *No, she's not.* And then she asked me how we got tickets. I said: *Well, my wife does things with the team.*"

I asked, "Is Jocelyn on the team?"

"No, her roommate's on the squad."

Like I said, in Texas it's two degrees of separation.

As far as the performance, I think he was a bit intimidated by the whole thing. The cheerleaders were on stage dancing in their uniforms, doing a lot of different routines with lots of costume changes, including red, white, and blue duds for a *Star-Spangled Banner* skit. It was a high-energy, fast-paced ninety-minute show with kicks flying everywhere, head swings, synchronized splits, complex formations— he didn't have time to think.

When it was over he was impressed. "Wow! That's a lot of talent. It must have been hard to get there, to make it onto that stage. It can't be easy to be a Cowboys Cheerleader. The kicks and the way they move ... I'm surprised they don't kick or run into each other. How do they do this?"

I looked at him. "It's very choreographed."

He was kind of awestruck by that. And I think he gained respect for the cheerleaders and their professionalism. They were obviously hard-working and talented and something to aspire to. The show was also very exciting and fun, so I think he better understood why it appealed to me. And I suspect part of him felt sorry for me, because he knows I didn't have much of a childhood.

Poor thing ... at least let her live out her childhood whenever she gets a chance. Her mother never really let her be around these teenage kids; this'll be her chance to do that.

I do think that's how he sees it. That I'm reliving the childhood I never had. And I do each time I walk through those doors and into the stadium.

Judge Kristi Scales' Tip for Auditions [29, 30]

★ Watch videos of the cheerleaders to study their dance style.

★ Work on building stamina by doing cardio at least four times a week.

★ Experiment with hair and makeup to find a look that enhances your natural beauty.

★ Start working on eating well-balanced meals to keep your body energized. No crash dieting or fasting!

★ No tube tops. Your choreography should not include using your hands to continually pull up your tube top, so choose a more appropriate outfit for auditions.

★ Spit out your chewing gum. It's really unbecoming.

★ Remove belly rings or body piercings. Do you want us to notice your high cheekbones and fabulous high kicks, or be distracted by a piece of metal extending from your eyebrow, lip, or nose?

★ Remove potentially embarrassing photos from your social media. You do not want Kelli Finglass or Charlotte Jones asking you about the photos of you at the Mardi Gras parade flashing for beads. Remember, if you're a Dallas Cowboys Cheerleader, you're an ambassador not only for our football team, but for our community. So please go through all your postings and photos and ask yourself: Is this in-line with the image of America's Sweethearts?

★ Know your stuff. Many people think it doesn't require any skill to be a cheerleader so when they show up to the open call audition they are often surprised. Professional cheerleading requires an extensive background in dance. In most cases, you must have knowledge in jazz, pom, and hip-hop. The Dallas Cowboys Cheerleaders incorporate all three dance styles in addition to stunting, tumbling, and even lyrical.

Remember, the judges are rooting for you, not against you. By showing up for auditions and doing your best, you've already won. So good for you.

Waiting in line while security checks the participants in. I always dress for success when arriving for tryouts.

You can never be too limber for the routine.

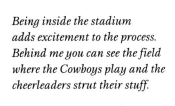

Being inside the stadium adds excitement to the process. Behind me you can see the field where the Cowboys play and the cheerleaders strut their stuff.

Interviewed by NBC5DFW reporter Jeff Smith, at the Powerhouse School of Dance *for the filming and interview.*

You can never be too limber for the routine.

Chapter 9

(Not) Making the Team

Saturday, May 14, 2016, finally arrived. I drove to the Sheraton on Friday night and tried to get to sleep by 10:30–11:00 but never really fell into a deep sleep. It was more like dozing because every little sound down the hallway woke me up. Then it was too humid, too hot, and I just kept getting up. At 4:30 a.m. I thought: *It's time to get up anyway,* and was out of bed before the alarm rang.

It was interesting because I had brought some food with me and after being starved for the past few weeks, I wasn't hungry at all, but I made myself eat a little bit of oatmeal anyway. I also kept checking my weather app because it was thundering and raining. I had an umbrella in my car, but it didn't really keep the rain off you that well, so I ended up buying a poncho in the hotel gift shop before I checked out around 6:30.

As usual, lots of people were already there when I pulled in. I got in line and saw a lot of mothers waiting with their daughters. You could already feel the electricity. I just love that tension of anticipation, my palms sweating. And of course the TV cameras were there already as well. I had a shower cap in my toiletries and put it on over my hair, which was in rollers because the rain was really coming down hard. Every year we've had to wait outside of the stadium for about an hour, so I was all prepared in my shower cap, cheap black vinyl poncho, and flimsy umbrella.

Ah, the glamorous life.

This time we only waited outside in the rain for like fifteen minutes. I was so glad when they opened the doors for us to go in around 7:15 because the rain was so bad. The storm had developed at the last minute, so no one was anticipating a deluge. But once we got inside, it was okay. Back when I first started coming they'd take your picture as you entered to verify your identity. Now it is all digitized. They match your driver's license with the DMV and before you show up they do background checks on all the participants. In the old days you could show up on a whim, pay your fee, and tryout. You could literally do a walk-up. Now you have to be pre-screened at least a week ahead of time.

I think in the past they had people make it all the way to the finals before finding out they had some kind of criminal record, which of course does not fit with the DCC's whole America's Sweethearts image. So instead of an open audition with a thousand people, there's probably half that many who have been pre-approved.

Once inside I recognized some of the girls who had tried out last year and they recognized me too. It was like: *Hey, you're back again.* They handed out our numbers—I was 63—and then around 8:00 we started stretching and getting in our positions. I was looking at all these girls around me, who were from all over the US, and they're gorgeous. Just like at my first audition, I felt like I had stumbled into a beauty pageant.

At 9:00 they instructed us to get in our seats and announced they had started filming. We sat there for about twenty or thirty minutes, then they took us to the actual stadium stands downstairs where Kelli Finglass, the director, gives her little introductory speech. CMT of course was there filming her.

She starts her remarks and at one point says, "This year we have several countries represented. We have Japan, we have Taiwan ..."

And I was like: *Oh yeah, Kelli; that's me, right here.*

"And we also have diverse careers ..." She went through a list: students, teachers, yadda, yadda, yadda, then added, "and also this year we have an author."

Everyone was looking around, and no one knew it was me.

During her introduction the year before she had mentioned, "I want to inspire women to achieve their goals. We have a variety of ages represented; our youngest is still in high school, and our oldest contestant, believe it or not, is forty-nine."

I looked around along with everybody, acting like I was trying to figure out who that fortysomething person was. Nobody zeroed in on me, and I gave a silent: Yes!

After that they brought us back up to the platform area where the auditions are held and we settled into our seats. Later on, one young lady pointed to a woman getting ready to tryout and said, "Hey, maybe that's the forty-nine-year-old up there."

And I shrugged. "*Hmm ...* maybe." And maybe not.

They have alumni cheerleaders help herd the participants to their seats, to the stage, wherever. One alumnus was Shelly Bramhall, who started with me in '99. From that first tryout she referred to me as Doc, which was weird, considering. So when I saw her this time she said, "Doc, you've got this down by now."

I told her, "Shelly, it's still nerve-wracking. My palms are sweating."

She laughed. "Just pat your hip and hit yourself on the butt."

But once I got up there, we were in rows of five and the judges were *that* close. So Kelli Finglass was there, and the choreographer Judy Trammell, and they recognized me because I'm the only one that keeps coming year after year.

Before we start everyone has to introduce themselves. So the first girl says her name is Suzie, she has ballet experience, is from San Jose, and is twenty-three.

Ye gods ...

The second girl was the captain of her drill team. She finished and handed the microphone to me. I looked at all the judges and saw the ones I've seen before smile back at me. There were some new judges, and they didn't give me any response.

In a very calm voice I said, "I'm Dr. Chiufang Hwang. I am a physician, wife, mother, and author. I am currently working on my second book entitled *Journey from Taiwan*, which is the country where I was born. But the United States of America is my homeland."

And everybody applauded, which I completely didn't expect. No one applauds the introductions. I guess it was because I said the United States was my homeland—this is Texas after all.

When the introductions were done, they staggered us three in front and two in back. And then it was time. The ninety seconds that I had worked so hard to prepare for. The music started, and I went into my routine. I was very nervous, and as I was going through it I was thinking: *Oh, my God, this is the longest ninety seconds.* I kept going over and over my routine, doing the kicks, splits, leaps, walk back, walk forward—everything. Then it was done.

At the end, you line up again and the camera pauses on each person's face from the chest up while the judges look at you on that big screen. When the camera was on me my lips were trembling so much from the intensity, and my throat was so dry. Afterwards when it was done, I walked off and went back to my seat and was so relieved. My palms immediately dried up, although the rest of me was soaked. And I was starving.

I said to the girl next to me, "I can't wait for lunch break."

And she whispered, "I can't wait to eat either."

They let us out for lunch about 1:30 and me and a couple other girls ran to the concession stand. I asked the guy, "Do you have a burger?"

Because it was Saturday they had a limited menu, so I had a barbecue sloppy joe. I sat with another girl who was eating tacos. We were too busy eating to even talk. I think I ate too fast because I got gastric reflux. I'm sure that doesn't fit the DCC image, either.

When our forty-five-minute lunch break was over, I walked back to my assigned seat feeling very full and a little bit chilled. But we had to keep on our tryout clothes while watching the rest of the girls perform. We also had to sit pretty and keep smiling throughout the day because the TV crew was filming the auditions, so you never knew when you'd be on camera. I smiled so much my jaws were about to lock up.

Last year when the audition episode of *Making the Team* aired I caught a glimpse of myself sitting in my row. Another time I was one of the girls walking by. This year was the first year they actually pulled me aside and interviewed me. After I auditioned the producer came up, and she called me over from my row. They took four of us downstairs and explained they were doing individual interviews. We figured there was something unique about us. The girl who was interviewed before me, for example, had skipped out on her college graduation to audition. Actually, I've heard a lot of girls say in the audition introduction, *I'm graduating from college today, but I'm not attending my commencement to be here.*

While waiting, I wondered what angle they wanted to use with me. When it was my turn, they brought me into the interview area, got me situated with the camera, then asked me where I was from. I told them I was born in Taiwan but was raised in the States.

"Why do you want to do this?"

"Well, I never had this in my culture. Even though I was living in the US, I didn't get to take dance. I didn't go to football games. It wasn't part of my parents' mindset or culture. And this gives me a chance to experience something quintessentially American."

"How many times have you tried out?"

"This is probably my tenth time."

"What are you trying to achieve?"

"I don't know."

"This is high performance. Have you performed before?"

"No. This is completely out of my comfort zone. That's what makes it unique. What also makes it unique is that I'm fifty."

She stared at me. "What?"

"I'm fifty, five-oh. My kids are twenty and twenty-three. I have twenty-one-year-olds sitting next to me, but to get myself in this kind of shape—to blend in for no one to question my age and no one to question my abilities when I come back each year to do the kick line, to do the routine, to do this—that's a goal for me. What I'm trying to achieve is fitting in."

I don't know if any or all of the interview will make it onto the show. Usually the audition episodes focus on the girls who make the team. Hence the name of the series. I didn't make the team, so I'll just have to wait and see.

Speaking of waiting, after the interview we went back to our seats and realized they had broken for lunch so that's when the other girl and I ran to the concession stand. We only had about twenty minutes to wolf down our food before having to be back in our seats for the afternoon auditions, which finished around four o'clock. They announced they would post the results at six o'clock, and at that point everyone just killed time while waiting. We can walk around and go to the bathroom or do whatever, but we have to stay inside the stadium. We cannot go outside the doors.

At six o'clock they let us go outside to see the posted numbers of the hundred or so girls who made it to the next round, and that's when all emotional hell breaks loose. Some girls are screaming for joy while others are hysterically crying. The vast majority just look glum. I'm always happy. I knew I didn't make the cut, but that's not really why I was there to begin with.

I looked around and noticed the gate by the parking lot. Behind it had to be two or three hundred mothers and friends waiting. The girl who had sat next to me all day said she'd come with her mother, who had planned to spend the day at the Marriott laying out by the pool. Fortunately for her, the sun had come out after the storm passed.

Every time the numbers are posted I always think: *Thank God my number's not posted because I don't know what I'd do if it was.* It would mean coming back the next day at 7:00 a.m. again and they teach you a routine on the field in the morning and that afternoon you have to perform it in front of the judges. I can't learn that fast; I have to memorize it. And it takes me months to memorize anything.

I'll be honest, in my daydreams I sometimes wonder if they'll post my number and pull me aside to make me some kind of inspirational figure. I know they won't pick me for the squad, but maybe they could use me as an ambassador. That would be a real dream. And something I would excel at.

Anyway, the girls who make the Sunday night cut come back the following Friday, for a one-on-one interview with Kelli. Then Saturday and Sunday are the finals. That's when you compete against the girls on the current squad. What's interesting is that if you used to be on the squad but either left or were cut, you have to start all over in the preliminaries again. Only current cheerleaders are grandfathered into the finals.

Those girls who make it will spend the entire summer rehearsing from 7:00 to 10:00 p.m. Monday through Friday learning their stuff. They start with forty-six candidates, but the squad gets weeded down each week—they get kicked off the cheerleader island, as it were—so by the time football season starts they'll have a squad of thirty-six.

It really is taking on a second career, one that doesn't pay in terms of immediate cash in hand since they only get fifty dollars per game. And nothing for all the rehearsals. But a lot of the younger girls are supported by their parents. Beyond not making any money, it's got to be exhausting, and it's definitely a huge commitment. But for many of the girls they see it as their ticket to the next step. It's a great résumé-builder.

They also have what's called the Show Group, which is an elite group that performs all over. Every year twelve to sixteen of the DCC's best dancers are selected to be part of the Show Group. These are the ladies that show up for meet-and-greets at various public events, from charity telethons to state fairs. They also perform a special musical variety show called *America & Her Music* at conventions and corporate events. But the group is most famous for supporting American troops.

Kelli says, "The reaction of the military to the Dallas Cowboys Cheerleaders USO tours has been a perfect marriage of cause and contribution on our part that I think an organization could ever have. We did our first USO tour in 1979 to Korea. Anywhere American soldiers are stationed, we've probably traveled there and entertained. It's a grueling schedule, but it's the most rewarding thing that any cheerleader could ever do. The reaction has always been very, very well-received. In fact, if we didn't have football games, we probably would do the USO tours full time because we can't even keep up with the demand. It's something very special to our organization."[31]

I think many of the girls auditioning really have an eye towards making the show group because they get the most publicity. There's a lot of ambition in the room during tryouts, a lot of dreams on the line. That's part of what makes the day so electric. The results can change lives. In my case, just being there, just participating, has changed me for the better.

Usually after the audition day is over, I would wake up the next morning a little depressed. Not because I hadn't made the cut but that it was over for that year. In 2015 for some reason I came crashing down really hard. Someone even joked before this audition: *We need to get you a mattress for when you crash after your audition.* But I think they misunderstood the root of my malaise. The letdown wasn't borne from not making the cut; it was that the regimented workout and preparation schedule was over. For now.

Once that discipline goes away, you just feel a bit of a void. I'll still work out seven days a week. It won't be nearly as intense; I'll swim and do other exercises just as religiously. The tryouts may happen only once a year, but my RA is a daily battle.

This year I was exhausted by the time I got home; it really is a long day with a lot of adrenaline and nerves. But the letdown in the days that followed was much milder. It was more of a wistfulness. I think all the press I did that hopefully inspired others, had elevated my mood so much that the letdown of the prep routine being over wasn't that big this year. I was able to better appreciate the accomplishment.

Before, my goal was to see how many TV interviews I could get, how many print press interviews I could get. I love to go after a reporter and ask: *Hey, do you want an interview?* This year I was more focused on doing a book on my experiences with the Dallas Cowboys Cheerleaders auditions and the reasons for it.

It was never my goal to be an actual Dallas Cowboys Cheerleader. Not in 1999 and not in 2016. I'm very pragmatic and I'm very realistic. And even if I had been selected back when I was thirty-four, I could not have accepted it. I have too much going on in my life. It would have been a thrill, and I would have felt so accomplished, but then I would have declined.

Like I said, this has always been about the journey, never actually making the team. And the journey isn't over.

How to Create an Awesome Solo Routine [32]

In 2015 teenager Holly P. auditioned for the DCC and made the squad on her first try. Here are some of the secrets to her success.

You have to practice your solo with full confidence all the time, every time, because you can't fake it. It has to be real and come from a real place. I suggest practicing everything: practice your facial expressions, practice your attitude. In your mind, pretend that Kelli and Judy are in front of you and pretend you're performing for them.

I video myself, and I would really suggest that you video yourself. If I look like I'm dull, I'll amp it up. If I look like I'm too amped, I'll bring it back down. It's all about being aware. In regards to video, there's even a slo-mo on iPhones. If you watch yourself and there's a move you don't like, you can put it in slo-mo and see your technique. You can see what you're doing wrong and what you're doing right. That's why it's definitely handy to use video.

If you don't have access to video, at least you can watch yourself in the mirror. What you think looks best for you is typically what others think will look best. You have to be very aware of yourself so that you know what is too much and what's not enough. You have to find that fine line and that fine line, really, is what you're comfortable with.

Chapter 10

Same Time, Next Year

It's been more than a month since the auditions, and I've been surprised at some of the responses I've gotten. People seem to appreciate my persistence and the discipline and dedication participating in the tryouts requires. Year after year. It's like they recognize that it's all about self-fulfillment rather than an end game.

And I'm already starting to plan for next year. My dance studio is on hiatus for part of the summer, but once they offer classes again I'll start attending different evening classes. I have to decide if I want to hire the same trainers or look for new people for a fresh outlook. I think when you're dealing with a creative endeavor, people get complacent as far as developing their style. I've noticed some choreographers start relying on the same move or combinations. They stop experimenting or stretching creatively. They essentially start phoning it in. So you don't always want to stick with the same style. You want to pick the best that you can hire, someone who challenges you and gets you excited.

Usually I pick someone that's already teaching at that studio because I'm familiar with them. And trust me, there are a lot of dancers out there to pick from. But using someone from the studio brings consistency. Someone can be the best choreographer in the world but if they're not consistent, if they don't come every week, if they can't communicate with you, if they're off auditioning in another city or country when they're supposed to be with you, then it won't work. They need to be available. Especially in my case because I don't have what you'd call natural talent.

For the most part, I know instructors employed by the studio show up every week. And I do my own vetting before approaching someone. I'll look at how frequently they show up and how many classes they are responsible for. I look at their style, how they dance, how they interact with the class, and then I hone in.

I usually say, "I would like to hire you for private lessons once a week for the next six months to teach a routine I'll use to try out for the Dallas Cowboys Cheerleaders."

I really do like shaking things up, so I don't use the same choreographer every year. Kelli and Judy have been watching my routines for years now, and I've got to give them something new. I have to live up to their expectations of me to be more professional every year. I can't let them down. I'll make the decision on who my next choreographer will be by September.

After taking it relatively easy for a few weeks after tryouts, in June I started working on stretching and flexibility again. I'm already thinking about what kind of routine I want to try. By October I'll be busy learning the routine—always an adventure. It usually takes me through November to learn the full routine. This is why I need a choreographer who shows up; I need a lot of one-on-one attention. Starting in December I'll continue rehearsing week after week so that by January the routine is clean and ready to go.

One of the other first things I do is choose my outfits for the next audition. I asked the dance instructors at Power House what apparel they used for their recitals. Someone suggested I check out the web site for Triple Threat Dancewear. I ended up purchasing a top from each of the three collections they offered.

However, there is always a danger with ordering clothes online. One of the tops I ordered had so many sequins on it that after wearing it I looked like I was on the short end of an encounter with an angry tabby. I was scratched all over. Some of the scratches took more than a week to heal. So that top was permanently retired.

For the audition, they specify you need to wear short shorts. But one pair I bought were so short as to be underwear. There was no way I could wear those in public. Under a tutu, maybe. But I wasn't trying out for the Bolshoi. So those shorts joined the sequined top.

You wouldn't think finding a pair of shorts and bustier would be that hard. Considering how little material they use. But the outfit style needs to flatter your body type and the color needs to complement your complexion. I check to see if I'm comfortable—no chafing or scratching—and if I have freedom of movement. You don't want to worry that your boobs are going to fall out.

So the wardrobe search starts in November. By December I have it all ironed out, and by January I have three of the same tops, which are a halter top style that shows your midriff. I'll have four pairs of hosiery and three pairs of short shorts, which we call booty shorts. And two pairs of shoes.

In past years I've gotten my photo together in December, but I already have my photo ready for next year's application. Also in December, I'll start looking online to see when in January I can sign up for the 2017 tryouts. One section of the application asks why you want to try out. Each year I answer a little differently. I don't know who, if anyone, reads it, but I try to put some thought into it. I think next year I'll say to celebrate the completion of my third book.

The prep classes will also get posted in January. When those start I'll resume the more intensive workouts, my kick instruction, and eventual total blockout—the process just repeats itself, all culminating in the tryouts next May.

I was thinking about the *Guinness Book of World Records*. I think the oldest person to audition for the DCC was a sixty-four-year-old.

I think it would be fun to surpass her then submit it to Guinness as the oldest candidate for an NFL cheerleading squad. There are always new goals to strive for, no matter how whimsical.

The thing is, with every decade that goes by, people are healthier. People are out there doing more. In 2013 an eighty-year-old man from Japan climbed Mt. Everest. In 2011 a one-hundred-year-old great-grandfather ran a marathon in Toronto. A seventy-one-year-old equestrian, also from Japan, competed in the 2012 Summer Olympics in London. Fifty years ago there would never have been a fifty-year-old trying out for a professional sports cheerleading squad.

We take better care of ourselves now. We know more. At least we know what we're supposed to do. So right now, as far as I'm concerned, there's really no end in sight. This is something I'm going to keep doing. I love the competition. I love seeing my improvement year to year. It might be incremental, but it's there. And that spurs me to keep trying to get even better.

Two years ago I noticed on the application we fill out online—everything is done digitally now—that in the box where you list your age, it stopped at forty-nine years old. In 2016, when I submitted in January I was still forty-nine—I turned fifty in March—but in 2017, they won't have my age listed. I guess I'll be forty-nine forever now.

Now, the DCC makes it clear there is no upper limit. Kelli has said she's there to empower women so why would they have an age cutoff. I also read an article by Kristi Scales, a sideline reporter for the Dallas Cowboys Radio Network, that said: "There is no maximum age. Heck, a few years ago we had a fifty-five-year-old and a sixty-two-year-old try out. And there's no gender requirement. So, in anticipation of your question, yes, we've had a man try out! That was several years ago. He was actually a very good dancer (a professional dance instructor, if I remember correctly), but he may not have looked too good wearing the short-shorts of the official DCC uniform."[33]

I actually know the guy she's talking about. His name is Sharpie and he was a high-kick instructor at Powerhouse. And my guess is he would totally rock the short shorts.

But seriously, I've been thinking about that application question for two years. Anyone who happened to be fifty and decided to go for it might be put off applying because some (twenty-one-year-old) computer programmer arbitrarily stopped at forty-nine.

All I want is the opportunity to audition for as long as I want to. For as long as I am physically able to. For as long as it challenges me. And for as long as it inspires me. Because then maybe I can inspire others to follow their dreams, however improbable.

You will never be sorry you did.

Notes

1. "Yale and Princeton Game Today," *New York Times*, June 22, 1909.

2. Bill Velasco, "NCC Nationals: Continuing a Rich Tradition," *Philippine Star*, February 23, 2015.

3. Hess, Amanda. "The Year Cheerleaders Fought Back," Slate, Dec. 23, 2004. http://www.slate.com/blogs/xx_factor/2014/12/23/nfl_cheerleading_football_teams_should_start_respecting_the_sport.html.

4. "The Broadening Curriculum," *New York Times*, Jan. 25, 1924.

5. Joe Nick Patoski, "The Original Dallas Cowboys Cheerleaders," *Texas Monthly*, Sept. 2001. http://www.texasmonthly.com/the-culture/the-original-dallas-cowboy-cheerleaders/.

6. Julia Lurie, "A Not-So-Brief and Extremely Sordid History of Cheerleading," *Mother Jones*, December 15, 2014.

7. Ibid.

8. John M. Crew Dson, "Cheering for the Cowboys," *New York Times*, April 19, 1978.

9. Ibid.

10. Lurie, *Mother Jones*.

11. Hudson Morgan, "She Packs Serious Heat On-Screen and Off—Person of Interest's Sarah Shahi Has Killer Looks and One Disarming Grin," CBS.com, Sept 24, 2014. http://www.cbs.com/shows/watch_magazine/archive/1003189.

12. Ibid.

13. "DCC History." *DallasCowboys.com*.

14. Heather Higgins, "Oh Pioneers: The Dallas Cowboys Cheerleaders," ColumbiaSportsJournalism.com, July 1, 2010. http://columbiasportsjournalism.com/2010/07/01/oh-pioneers.

15. Patoski, *Texas Monthly*.

16. Tania Canedo, "Looking After America's Sweethearts: An Interview with Kelli Finglass," *AmstarDMC.com*, April 8, 2015. https://www.amstardmc.com/blog/interview-kelli-finglass/.

17. Warren Allan, "Looking After America's Sweethearts: An Interview with Kelli Finglass." *UltimateCheerleader.com*, April 2015. http://ultimatecheerleaders.com/2015/04/looking-after-americas-sweethearts-an-interview-with-kelli-finglass.

18. TCA Press conference, July 2007.

19. TCA press conference, July 2007.

20. Jeryl Brunner, "Inside the Hit TV Show *Dallas Cowboys Cheerleaders: Making the Team*," *Huffington Post*, Oct. 21, 2013. http://www.huffingtonpost.com/jeryl-brunner/dallas-cowboys-cheerleaders-making-the-team_b_4138481.html.

21. TCA press conference, July 2007.

22. Jennifer Acosta Scott, "The Link Between Rheumatoid Arthritis and Diabetes," *Everyday Health*, July 31, 2013. http://www.everydayhealth.com/rheumatoid-arthritis/living-with/the-link-between-rheumatoid-arthritis-and-diabetes.

23. http://chiufang.com/news/.

24. Leslie Barker, "Watch a 50-year-old Doctor Train with Teens for Her Shot at Being a Dallas Cowboys Cheerleader," Dallas Morning News, Apr 18, 2016. http://www.dallasnews.com/lifestyles/health-and-fitness/columnists/leslie-barker/20160418-watch-a-50-year-old-doctor-train-with-teens-for-her-shot-at-being-a-dallas-cowboys-cheerleader.ece.

25. "Gussie Nell Davis," *Texas State Historical Association*, Dallas Morning News, December 21, 1993. Notable Women of Texas, 1984–85 (Irving, Texas: Emerson Publishing, 1984). Texas Star, November 14, 1971. Vertical Files, Dolph Briscoe Center for American History, University of Texas at Austin.

26. Scales, 5poinstblue.com.

27. Ojeda, Louis Jr., "Doctor Never Quits Trying to Become Cowboys Cheerleader," FOX Sports Southwest, May 04, 2015. http://www.foxsports.com/southwest/story/dallas-cowboys-cheerleaders-auditions-doctor-never-gives-up-050415.

28. Miles, CBSDFW.

29. Kristi Scales, "A Judge's Handy-Dandy Tips for Dallas Cowboys Cheerleaders Auditions," 5pointsblue.com, Apr 28th, 2015. http://www.5pointsblue.com/a-judges-handy-dandy-tips-for-dallas-cowboys-cheerleaders-auditions/.

30. "Audition Tips," cheertime101.com, http://cheertime101.com/audition-tips-3.

31. TCA press conference, July 2007.

32. Kristi Scales, "Countdown to DCC Finals: Holly P's Advice for an Awesome Solo Routine," *5pointsblue.com*, May 19th, 2016. http://www.5pointsblue.com/countdown-dcc-finals-holly-ps-advice-awesome-solo-routine.

33. Scales, "A Judge's Handy-Dandy Tips."

Bibliography

A

"About DCC." *CMT.com.* http://cmtdallascowboyscheerleaders.blogspot.com/p/auditions.html.

Allan, Warren. "Looking After America's Sweethearts: An Interview with Kelli Finglass." *UltimateCheerleader.com,* April 2015. http://ultimatecheerleaders.com/2015/04/looking-after-americas-sweethearts-an-interview-with-kelli-finglass/.

"Auditions Dallas Cowboys Cheerleaders." *DallasCowboys.com.* http://www.dallascowboys.com/content/auditions-dallas-cowboys-cheerleaders.

"Audition FAQs." *DallasCowboys.com.* 2016. http://www.dallascowboys.com/content/auditions-faq.

"Audition Tips." *cheertime101.com.* http://cheertime101.com/articles/.

B

Barker, Leslie. "Watch a 50-year-old Doctor Train with Teens for Her Shot at Being a Dallas Cowboys Cheerleader." *Dallas Morning News,* Apr 18, 2016. http://www.dallasnews.com/lifestyles/health-and-fitness/columnists/leslie-barker/20160418-watch-a-50-year-old-doctor-train-with-teens-for-her-shot-at-being-a-dallas-cowboys-cheerleader.ece.

Battaglia, Joe. "Angela VanDeWalle: Memoir of a Dallas Cowboys Cheerleader (with video from audition)." *FloCheer.com.* November 24, 2015. http://www.flocheer.com/article/37576-angela-vandewalle-memoir-of-a-dallas-cowboys-cheerleader.

Betsill, Jay. Dallas Cowboys Cheerleaders 2013 auditions at Cowboys Stadium." *DFW.com.* May 7, 2013. http://www.dfw.com/2013/05/07/791378/dallas-cowboys-cheerleaders-2013.html.

Betsill, Jay. "Dallas Cowboys Cheerleaders 2015 auditions at AT&T Stadium." *DFW.com.* May 11, 2015. http://www.dfw.com/2015/05/11/994254/dallas-cowboys-cheerleaders-2015.html.

Braswell, Sean. "The Cowboys' New Cheerleaders." YahooNews.com. Nov. 26, 2015. http://www.ozy.com/flashback/the-cowboys-new-cheerleaders/33985.

Brunner, Jeryl. "Inside the Hit TV Show *Dallas Cowboys Cheerleaders: Making the Team.*" *Huffington Post,* Oct. 21, 2013. http://www.huffingtonpost.com/jeryl-brunner/dallas-cowboys-cheerleaders-making-the-team_b_4138481.html.

C

Canedo, Tania. "Looking After America's Sweethearts: An Interview with Kelli

Finglass." *AmstarDMC.com*. April 8, 2015. https://www.amstardmc.com/blog/interview-kelli-finglass/.

Ciesco, Tim. "2016 Dallas Cowboys Cheerleader Auditions." NBCDFW.com. May 7,2016.http://www.nbcdfw.com/blogs/blue-star/Dallas-Cowboys-Cheerleader-Auditions_Dallas-Fort-Worth-378487866.html.

D

"The Dallas Cowboys Cheerleaders." *Internet Archive Wayback Machine*. https://web.archive.org/web/20070204024244/http://www.dallascowboys.com/cheerleaders/history.cfm.

"Dallas Cowboys Cheerleaders—History." YouTube video. July 6, 2014. https://www.youtube.com/watch?v = ODXzf2SoBwI.

"Dallas Cowboys Cheerleaders Legend Suzanne Mitchell Continues to Give Back." *CheerChannel*.com. April 4, 2014. http://www.cheerchannel.com/videos/dallas-cowboys-cheerleaders-legend-suzanne-mitchell-continues-to-give-back.

Dallas Cowboys Cheerleaders: Making the Team. TV series. CMT.

Dallas Cowboys Cheerleaders: Making the Team. Television Critics Association press conference. July 2007.

"Dallas Cowboys Cheerleaders: Pictures and History." *YourDailyCowboysFootball Fix.com* . http://yourdailycowboysfootballfix.com/portfolio/dallas-cowboys-cheerleaders-pictures-history/.

"DCC History." DallasCowboys.com. http://www.dallascowboys.com/content/dcc-history.

Dingus, Anne. "Texas Primer: The Dallas Cowboys Cheerleaders." *Texas Monthly*. Jan 1998. http://www.texasmonthly.com/the-culture/texas-primer-the-dallas-cowboys-cheerleaders/.

Dingus, Anne. "The Dallas Cowboys Cheerleaders." *Texas Monthly*. Feb. 7, 2009.

Dson, John M. Crew. "Cheering for the Cowboys." *New York Times,* April 19, 1978. "Interview with Brandi Nace, Vonciel Baker." Transcript from *CNN Sunday Morning. CNN.com*. Aired September 15, 2002. http://transcripts.cnn.com/TRANSCRIPTS/0209/15/sm.06.html.

E

Evans, Mary. *A Decade of Dreams*. Dallas, TX: Taylor Publishing, 1982.

G

Gussie Nell Davis." Texas State Historical Association, Dallas Morning News, December 21, 1993. Notable Women of Texas, 1984–85 (Irving, Texas: Emerson Publishing, 1984). Texas Star, November 14, 1971. Vertical Files, Dolph Briscoe Center for American History, University of Texas at Austin.

H

Hess, Amanda. "The Year Cheerleaders Fought Back." *Slate*, Dec. 23, 2004. http://

www.slate.com/blogs/xx_factor/2014/12/23/nfl_cheerleading_football_teams_should_start_respecting_the_sport.html.

Higgins, Heather. "Oh Pioneers: The Dallas Cowboys Cheerleaders." *ColumbiaSportsJournalism.com.* July 1, 2010. http://columbiasportsjournalism.com/2010/07/01/oh-pioneers/.

"History of the Dallas Cowboys' Cheerleaders." *ESPN.com.* http://www.dallascowboys.com/content/dcc-history.

K

Kast, Catherine. "The History of the Dallas Cowboys Cheerleaders Look." *People Style,* August 25, 2016. http://site.people.com/style/the-history-of-the-dallas-cowboys-cheerleaders-look/today.

"Kelli Finglass, Director, Dallas Cowboys Cheerleaders." *CMT.com.* http://www.cmt.com/show/dallas_cowboys_cheerleaders/season_7/cast_member.jhtml?personalityId=14266#moreinfo.

L

Litman, Laken. "Five Things You Need to Know about the Dallas Cowboys Cheerleaders' Reality TV Show." USAToday.com. Aug 8, 2014. http://ftw.usatoday.com/2014/08/5-things-you-need-to-know-about-the-dallas-cowboys-cheerleaders-reality-tv-show..

Lurie, Julia. "A Not-So-Brief and Extremely Sordid History of Cheerleading." *Mother Jones.* December 15, 2014.

M

McNab, Heather. "Homesickness, training five nights a week AND a full time job! Aussie girl Jinelle Esther reveals what it takes to be a Dallas Cowboy Cheerleader... and she loves it." *Daily Mail Australia.* December 21, 2014. http://www.dailymail.co.uk/news/article-2882402/It-feels-incredible-love-Aussie-girl-Jinelle-Esther-reveals-life-Dallas-Cowboy-Cheerleader.html#ixzz4JxmjmKlE

Miles, JD. "49-Year-Old Auditions for Dallas Cowboys Cheerleaders." *CBSDFW.com.* May 8, 2015. http://dfw.cbslocal.com/2015/05/08/49-year-old-auditions-for-dallas-cowboys-cheerleaders/.

Mitchell, Suzanne. *Dallas Cowboys Cheerleaders: A Touch of Class.* New York: Jordan & Company, 1979.

Morgan, Hudson. "She Packs Serious Heat On-Screen and Off—Person of Interest's Sarah Shahi Has Killer Looks and One Disarming Grin." *CBS.com.* Sept 24, 2014. http://www.cbs.com/shows/watch_magazine/archive/1003189/.

Morris, Kate. "Life with the Dallas Cowboys Cheerleaders." *DanceSpiritMagazine.com.* Feb 4, 2009. http://www.dancespirit.com/how-to/dance-team/life_with_the_dallas_cowboys_cheerleaders.

Morse, Kristen Green. "Dallas Cowboys Cheerleaders." *Sports Illustrated,* July 2, 2001.

O

Ojeda, Louis Jr. "Behind the Scenes at Dallas Cowboys Cheerleaders Auditions." *FOX Sports Southwest*, May 03, 2015. http://www.foxsports.com/southwest/photos/dallas-cowboys-cheerleaders-auditions-050215.

Ojeda, Louis Jr. "Doctor Never Quits Trying to Become Cowboys Cheerleader." *FOX Sports Southwest*, May 04, 2015. http://www.foxsports.com/southwest/story/dallas-cowboys-cheerleaders-auditions-doctor-never-gives-up-050415.

P

Patoski, Joe Nick. "The Original Dallas Cowboys Cheerleaders." *Texas Monthly*, Sept. 2001.

S

Scales, Kristi. "2015 Dallas Cowboys Cheerleaders Auditions Begin May 2nd in Arlington." *Arlington.org.* Apr 27, 2015. http://www.arlington.org/plan/blog/post/2015-dallas-cowboys-cheerleaders-auditions-begin-may-2nd-in-arlington/.

Scales, Kristi. "A Judge's Handy-Dandy Tips for Dallas Cowboys Cheerleaders Auditions." *5pointsblue.com.* Apr 28th, 2015. http://www.5pointsblue.com/a-judges-handy-dandy-tips-for-dallas-cowboys-cheerleaders-auditions.

Scales, Kristi. "What Really Happens at Dallas Cowboys Cheerleaders Auditions?" 5PointsBlue.com. May 12, 2016. http://www.5pointsblue.com/really-happens-dallas-cowboys-cheerleaders-auditions.

Scales, Kristi. "Countdown to DCC Finals: Holly P's Advice for an Awesome Solo Routine." *5pointsblue.com.* May 19th, 2016. http://www.5pointsblue.com/countdown-dcc-finals-holly-ps-advice-awesome-solo-routine.

Scholz, Stephanie, and Sheri Scholz. *Deep in the Heart of Texas: Reflections of Former Dallas Cowboys Cheerleaders.* New York: St. Martin's Press, 1991.

Scott, Jennifer Acosta. "The Link Between Rheumatoid Arthritis and Diabetes." *Everyday Health*, July 31, 2013. http://www.everydayhealth.com/rheumatoid-arthritis/living-with/the-link-between-rheumatoid-arthritis-and-diabetes.

Shropshire, Mike. *The Ice Bowl.* New York: Donald I. Fine Books, 1997.

T

Television Critics Association press conference July 2007.

V

Velasco, Bill. "NCC Nationals: Continuing a Rich Tradition." *The Philippine Star*, February 23, 2015.

American Sweetheart:
Still Not Making the Team

Chiufang Hwang, M.D.

www.chiufang.com

Publisher: SDP Publishing
Also available in ebook format

Available at all major bookstores

www.SDPPublishing.com

Contact us at: info@SDPPublishing.com

CPSIA information can be obtained
at www.ICGtesting.com
Printed in the USA
FSOW02n0805170217
30810FS